The Anglo-Manxman

A LIFE OF A. W. MOORE

ARTHUR WILLIAM MOORE, ESQ., C.V.O., J.P.,
SPEAKER OF THE HOUSE OF KEYS, 1898-1909.

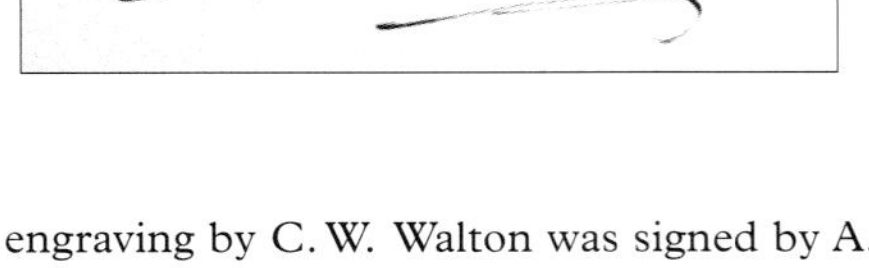

A proof copy of this engraving by C. W. Walton was signed by A. W. Moore in 1909.

The Anglo-Manxman

A life of A. W. Moore

Robert Fyson

Manx Heritage Foundation

Published by The Manx Heritage Foundation
PO Box 1986, Douglas, Isle of Man IM99 1SR

www.manxheritage.org

First published 2009

ISBN 978-0-9562064-2-8

British Cataloguing in Publication Data
A catalogue record for this book is available from the British Library

Printed and bound in Wales by Gomer Press Limited, Ceredigion

MANX HERITAGE FOUNDATION

For Valerie

AND IN MEMORY
OF MY MOTHER
DOROTHY FYSON
(1909-1990)

Acknowledgements

My first debt is to my partner Valerie Cottle, who typeset and laid this book out, acted as picture editor and research assistant, compiled the index, and in all sorts of ways made it possible, not least by feeding and harassing a slow and procrastinating author. William Moore, A. W. Moore's great-grandson, welcomed me to his home at Eton College, showed me family books, papers, photographs and paintings, and has been especially helpful in providing illustrative material. The staff at the Manx National Heritage Library have, as always, been very helpful: Wendy Thirkettle originally stimulated my interest with a talk she gave about Moore's diaries to the Isle of Man Victorian Society in 2002; Roger Sims, before he retired from MNH, acquired some papers of Canon John Quine's which have formed a crucial part of my research material; Alan Franklin and other staff have constantly helped with information and suggestions. Other archivists to whom I owe thanks include Jeremy Goldsmith (College of Heralds), Adam C. Green (Trinity College, Cambridge), Bobbie Judd (St Andrew's Healthcare, Northampton), Rusty Maclean (Rugby School) and Angharad Mair Jones (Gwynnedd Archives Service). Graham and Marina Warwick, by throwing their home open for a Victorian Society visit on a Sunday afternon, made it possible for me to visit Cronkbourne. Charles Guard of the Manx Heritage Foundation has been a tolerant and patient publisher. Ruth Sutherland has designed the cover and enhanced some of the archive photographs, John C. Hall did extra photography, and John G. Hall gave advice on heraldry. Finally, a large number of people interested in Manx history have helped in many ways by delving into their own knowledge. They include Fenella Bazin, Sandra Bolton, Frances Coakley, Ulla Corkill, Nigel Crowe, Belinda Drinkwater, Peter Farrant, Dollin Kelly, Dorothy Kelly, Peter Kelly, Laurie Kermode, Caroline McDonald, Pat Nicholson, Adrian Pilgrim and Sir David Wilson. My thanks to them all, and apologies to anyone I may have forgotten to mention. RF

Illustrations on pages 2, 18, 31, 32, 51, 63, 97, 103, 118, 119, 120, 125 and 146 have been reproduced by permission of Manx National Heritage; the portrait of Moore on page 108 by permission of the Gwynnedd Archives Service, and photographs on pages 17, 19, 20, 33, 34, 51, 52, 64, 65, 66, 67, 68 and 122 by courtesy of William Moore. John C. Hall photographed R. E. Morrison's portrait of A. W. Moore and the bust by Frank Mowbray Taubman (page 151) by permission of the Clerk of Tynwald.

CONTENTS

LIST OF *ILLUSTRATIONS*

PREFACE

The late nineteenth and early twentieth centuries were a period of great importance in the making of Manx national and cultural identity. Among the leading figures in this process were the poet T. E. Brown (1830-97), the novelist Hall Caine (1853-1931), the naturalist and archaeologist P. M. C. Kermode (1855-1932), the artist and designer Archibald Knox (1864-1933), and Sophia Morrison (1859-1917), pioneer of the Manx language revival movement. Arthur William Moore (1853-1909), the historian, writer and politician, was an equally influential figure.

A. W. Moore, as he is always known, remains, a century after his death, the outstanding historian of the Island. His *A History of the Isle of Man* (1900) in two volumes is still the standard work to which all subsequent historians must refer, a monument of late Victorian scholarship, its 1,000-odd pages never likely to be surpassed as a single-author, large-scale, history of the Island. He was also, from about 1885 onwards, a prolific writer on other Manx subjects, his books covering place names and surnames, folk-lore, ballads and music, and translations from the Manx language; these have been described as 'the foundation texts of Manx studies'.[1] Finally, Moore made a notable contribution to public and political life in the Island: elected to the House of Keys in 1885, he remained a member for the rest of his life, became Speaker in 1898, and in the early years of the twentieth century led the Keys' struggle for constitutional reform in the face of the intransigent diehard Governor, Lord Raglan.

For all these reasons, Moore is worth writing about. But he first attracted my interest because, among his surviving papers in the Manx National Heritage Library, there are two volumes of diaries, a valuable starting-point and primary source for a biographer.[2] These diaries are in some ways disappointing. The entries are usually brief, intermittent, and tersely factual. They do not cover all aspects of his life. For instance, there is little about the sailcloth factory which was the main source of the family income. In Moore's own words, speaking to his first biographer, his diary is 'a mere record of events as I could never bring myself to write down my thoughts'.[3]

Nevertheless I have relied heavily on the diaries in producing this account, which is intended primarily as a study of the man, rather than of the books he wrote.[4] I am very conscious that I am not an expert in most of the subjects that Moore addressed, and I have no knowledge of the Manx language. But close attention to his diaries has helped me, I hope, to understand and to portray the public and private worlds of this respectable, upper-middle class Victorian gentleman, who was equally at home, as my title suggests, in the Isle of Man and in England.

One other major source came to light just in time for me to make use of it. In the summer of 2008 Roger Sims, then senior archivist at Manx National Heritage, acquired for the Library an important accession of further papers of Canon John Quine. These included notes of Quine's conversations with Moore, interspersed with notes on both Moore's surviving diaries and his (now sadly missing) travel diaries, and an intriguing account of 'How Arthur Moore got to be Speaker of the House of Keys'.[5] Quine was a complex and contradictory character who deserves a biography of his own, for which I am now doing research.

Quine was aware of the difficulties facing the biographer. Writing about an earlier Moore, the Revd Philip (1705-83), in 1885, he gloomily pronounced judgement that 'Biography, in the modern sense, cannot be adequately written a century after the man's voice has become silent, and his face lost in the dimness of total oblivion. It is too late to hope now that the Reverend Philip Moore can be brought back to our view out of so vast a void. We live in a new era, as well as in a new century'.[6]

Writing a century after A. W. Moore's death, a century of even more rapid change than that which preceded it, I hope nevertheless to have achieved partial success in bringing Arthur William Moore 'back to our view out of so vast a void'.

Robert Fyson, Douglas, July 2009

Chapter 1

CHILDHOOD

Arthur Moore's earliest memories concerned his treatment by a cruel nurse before he was five. She used to turn him out of his pram and then push the front wheel against him to make him 'march'. At night she hung a rug behind his cot, telling him that it concealed a big black bear who would eat him if he did not go to sleep, as a result of which he suffered sleepless and terror-stricken nights. There were other minor cruelties, accompanied by threats of awful punishments if he told his parents, which he never dared to. He felt great joy at her departure in 1858, when she was replaced by Annie Cowin, his new nurse, whom he described as kind and good, and who was still employed at Cronkbourne more than fifty years later.[1]

On the occasion of his fifth birthday, little Arthur was disappointed at the postponement of a magic lantern show for the children of Cronkbourne, but was consoled by having gooseberry jam for tea. He also had early memories of wearing thin and inadequate clothes: a brown holland tunic and nankeen pants, with his legs left bare. Family pets were fondly recollected, especially a Newfoundland dog and a black-and-tan terrier.[2]

As with all children, as he grew older Arthur's fragmentary impressions of the world would become more securely located in an understanding of the family and social context in which he lived. From his earliest days he must have been impressed, even though he would have taken it for granted as being in the natural order of things, with his status as the eldest son in the Moore family of Cronkbourne.

The Moores had been in business as manufacturers since 1790, initially as linen millers and general merchants in Douglas, firstly in Society Lane near the harbour, and afterwards in Factory Lane, now Wellington Street.[3] Spinning, weaving and bleaching were all carried on, and the firm diversified from linen manufacture into sackcloth and sailcloth, which gradually became the mainstay of the family fortunes.

In early nineteenth-century Douglas, after the Napoleonic Wars, 'polite society' was dominated by a leisured elite of urban gentry, many of them half-pay military and naval officers and their families. According to one

Victorian memoir-writer, 'wealth was at a discount, and society was so exclusive, that anyone ever so remotely connected with trade aspired in vain to gain an entry into the privileged sets'.[4] However the rise of the Moores shows that upward social mobility was possible for at least one well-to-do family 'connected with trade'. A. W. Moore's father William Fine Moore (1814-1895) was born in Athol Street, Douglas, a prime residential address.

The crucial development in the Moores' social ascent took place in 1825 when James Moore (1772-1846), the head of the family and of the business, bought the estate of Ballafletcher. About two years later he built a mansion he named Cronkbourne, overlooking the River Glass and on a scale appropriate for members of the landed gentry, as the new family home.[5] It may have been at about this time that he started using a coat of arms similar to one claimed by the Moore family of More Hall and Bank Hall in Lancashire, although the connection was tenuous.[6] At Tromode, on the opposite side of the river, and about a quarter of a mile upstream, James Moore built an extensive new mill. Between the house and the mill, Cronkbourne Village – purpose-built to accommodate the mill's workforce – consisted of two rows of terraced cottages, forty-two in all. Industrial colony, factory and country house stood close to one another in what was by the mid-nineteenth century a flourishing concern, providing sailcloth to the Admiralty for the Royal Navy and also to merchant shipping. Brunel's famous iron steamship, the SS *Great Britain*, launched in Bristol in 1843, was equipped with sails made by Moore's of Tromode.[7]

In 1841, the year of the first household census, Cronkbourne was occupied by 'James Moore, merchant, 68' and his wife 'Elizabeth, gentlewoman, 65', together with their son William, also a 'merchant, 27', i.e. working in the family business. A small boy, four-year-old John Moore, whose relationship to the rest of the family is unclear, and four servants completed the tally of occupants. Ten years later, in 1851, the population of the house had shrunk: James and Elizabeth were both dead and William Fine Moore was living there alone, still unmarried, with just two female servants to look after him. The following year, however, William married, like his father before him, a woman living in England but with Isle of Man connections. Hannah Christian (1827-1914) lived in London before her marriage, but was a descendant of the Christians of Milntown and the Christian Curwens of Cumberland. The couple were married at St Mary's Church, Islington, on 29 April 1852, and their first child, Arthur William, was born nine months and one week later, on 6 February 1853, at Cronkbourne.

Arthur Moore's memories of his earliest years, as we have seen, were mainly concerned with the nursemaids who looked after him. From about the age of five, parents, family, other adults and events outside the home began to make a greater impression. He recalled the visits of his uncle, Archdeacon Joseph Moore (1802-86) and how the local clergy, including his godfather 'Parson' Drury (Revd William Drury, 1808-87, Vicar of Braddan from 1847 until his death), came to meet the Archdeacon at breakfast. The Moores were devoted Anglicans, and W. F. Moore's eldest brother Joseph, a lifelong bachelor who was Rector of Andreas and Archdeacon from 1844 until he died, was the object of especial reverence within the family. Other memories from young Arthur's childhood included his early reading matter, the appropriately-named *Little Arthur's History of England*, and a geography book called *Near Home*. He also remembered reading aloud to his father a report in *The Times* about the 1857 Indian Mutiny. He later read a ten-volume history of the mutiny, bought from an old soldier.

Arthur Moore venerated his father, in true Victorian style. Some impression of the character of William Fine Moore can be gleaned from a brief unpublished memoir entitled 'My Schooldays', which he wrote in 1892 when he was seventy-eight. He begins by reminiscing affectionately about his old Douglas teachers, Mr Imeson from Yorkshire, renowned for the teaching of mathematics at his own private academy, and the Revd Robert Brown, headmaster of Douglas Grammar School, a brilliant teacher of Latin and Greek, who was the father of T. E. Brown and later Vicar of Braddan. The account continues beyond Moore's schooldays, recalling how in December 1830, after he had left school, 'my parents thought it would do me good [to see] a little of the world before deciding upon my future course in life'. He travelled by stagecoach from Liverpool to London to spend six months with his mother Elizabeth's relatives. When he returned, his mother wanted him to go to university but, he modestly remarks, he thought it would be too expensive, and 'like a fond Parent, I think she entertained too high an opinion of her son's abilities'. William decided to stay at home and help his overworked father 'in conducting his manufacturing, agriculture, also the agency of the Sun Fire and Life Insurance Co. ... although under other circumstances I would gladly have embraced the ministry'.

Duty was William Fine Moore's watchword, and he recalls how 'I set to work and succeeded in opening a Sunday School at Cronkbourne on the 11th of August 1831, a circumstance which I shall ever remember with pleasure and satisfaction, now 61 years ago, because I believe it was instrumental in doing much good'. Later he opened, at his own expense, a Church of England elementary school in the village, which flourished for many years; he eventually handed it over to the Board of Education, but in 1892 they closed it and opened a new school at Kewaigue.[8]

There is much more that one would like to know about William Fine Moore. Surviving photographs show a sensitive and humorous face – perhaps more humorous than that of his illustrious eldest son. Susan Hicks Beach wrote in the 1950s that he was 'within memory as an elderly man, spare, active, open of countenance, kindly, and younger in spirit than his eldest son. Visitors in the house saw little of him, however, for affairs engrossed him'.[9] His memoir gives the impression of a philanthropic but essentially modest man, which is confirmed by the record of his public activities. He was a widely-respected public figure and an active and generous Church of England layman. He sat on the board of the Isle of Man Bank, of which he was a co-founder in 1865, the Steam Packet Company and the Electric Telegraph Company. In 1857 he had become both a magistrate and a member of the old unelected House of Keys. Espousing progressive views, and supporting the principle of popular election, he came top of the poll to represent Douglas in the first Keys election of 1867. Later in life he was largely responsible for the building of the new church at Braddan, consecrated in 1876, but he made it plain that he did not want to be commemorated by any memorial plaque or stained glass window. A Vice-President of the Manx Society for the Preservation and Publication of National Documents, founded in 1858, he evidently passed this interest on to young Arthur.[10]

William Fine Moore was a powerful example for his eldest son to follow. As is often the case with women in the past, it is more difficult to find out much about Hannah Moore. She took part in Sunday School teaching and other good works associated with the Church of England, for which she was praised in her obituaries. Mrs Hicks Beach described her as 'too sensible to be a spendthrift, but with a decided predilection for quality in life'. She was tall, slim and elegant, with a 'quietly rakish spirit', and capable of 'edged humour'. One unfavourable judgement was recorded in private, in 1898 or after, by an observer of the Moore family: John Quine wrote that A. W. Moore was 'selfish from a socially clever pitiless merciless mother'. Quine could be jaundiced, but there may have been an element of truth in his view. Hannah Moore, brought up in fashionable London, may have been more worldly, and ambitious on her son's behalf, than her husband.[11]

Arthur Moore was to be the eldest – eventually – of ten children, of whom only six enjoyed a full adult lifespan. Alfred James Moore died as an infant in 1855. The Moores' third son, Henry James, known as Harry, was born in 1856. Arthur Moore mentioned his birth in conversation with Quine, and his presence at Cronkbourne at the age of four is recorded in the 1861 census. According to A. R. W. Moore's history of the family, Harry suffered an accident falling out of a tree at Rugby School, but the Rugby archives have no record of this, or indeed of the presence of an H. J. Moore at the school. Whatever the truth of this, the story of Harry Moore is a tragedy which must have affected the whole family deeply. His death certificate, dated 18 February 1888, identifies him clearly as the son of W. F. Moore, merchant, of Cronkbourne, and states that he died at St Andrew's Hospital, Northampton, aged thirty-one, from erysipelas and diarrhoea. Further enquiries have revealed that St Andrew's, still a leading mental hospital today, was in Victorian times known as a modern, progressive lunatic asylum. Harry was admitted there in September 1877, aged twenty-one, suffering from dementia. The cause of his insanity was not known, but it was of long standing; he had been transferred there from The Priory, Roehampton, a similar institution where he had spent the previous three years. When he was admitted to St Andrew's he 'could not converse at all, did not know his age, and said yes to everything that was said to him'. Later he was described as 'childish and excitable', but well behaved, and perhaps able to read 'a little light literature'. Until his physical health began to fail in 1885, he was able to work in the garden and on the hospital farm.[12]

Harry Moore is not mentioned at all in his brother Arthur's diary. Mental illness was a taboo subject for many Victorians, and considered a stigma on one's family. W. F. Moore paid for Harry to live in one of the very best mental institutions of his day, but he was a long way from home.

Florence, born in 1860, died as a young woman of twenty-two. Ewan Douglas (1862-3) was another infant death. Edith (born 1858) and the four youngest children, Alice Dorothy (1865), Godfrey (1868) Margaret Rosamund ('Rosie', 1871) and Katie Mildred (1874), would all live to a good age. Arthur Moore's oldest sister was five years younger than him, his only surviving brother a full fifteen years younger, almost a different generation. This family pattern probably increased his sense of responsibility as the eldest child, and the main focus of his parents' hopes.

Despite family difficulties and the children's deaths, there seems no reason to doubt that Arthur Moore enjoyed a reasonably normal and happy childhood with his parents and three younger siblings, in a home staffed (in 1861) by a cook, a housemaid and two nursemaids. No doubt the memories he recalled in conversation with John Quine differed little from those of other comfortably brought-up children of his era: in 1859, smashing a carriage pulled by another boy by tobogganing it down a farmyard hill; having the whooping cough; and going on holiday with his family and his mother's sister, Aunt Jemima, to Llandudno, where they climbed a hill (probably the Great Orme) and ate winkles. In 1860 his new sister Florence was christened by Bishop Powys. In 1861 he admired the Volunteers and the Artillery on parade, led by Captain Joseph Jefferson of Bemahague – the beginning of a lifelong enthusiasm for military manoeuvres and shooting. He also remembered the deaths of his grandmother Christian, and of Prince Albert, which he heard announced when he was at a children's party at Kirby, home of the Drinkwater family. In 1863, due to alterations being undertaken at Cronkbourne, the family decamped for six months to live in lodgings in Derby Terrace, Douglas, later moving to another rented house in Christian Road to avoid an outbreak of typhoid fever. At home at Cronkbourne again, Arthur enjoyed owning both a donkey and a Shetland pony. His special friend was a little boy called Walter Kinder, who lived at Falcon Cliff, and they played with bows and arrows. On one occasion he was nearly drowned, sailing toy boats on the swollen River Glass.

Young Arthur attended a fête held to celebrate the marriage of the Prince of Wales, the future King Edward VII, and Princess Alexandra in March 1863. He took a great interest in races between the different Steam Packet boats, and also in naval battles in the American Civil War – especially when the Steam Packet vessel *Douglas* was sold to the Confederates as a blockade runner, sunk by a Northern ship but then raised and given a new lease of life as the *Gettysburg*. In 1864 he was involved in a fight himself, exchanging blows with George Drinkwater in defence of George's younger brother John. In later life, Arthur's recollections of the 1860s included crinolines and bustles, pictures of Garibaldi, the hero of Italian unification, and 'Dolly Vardon' hats.

In 1865, at the age of twelve and about to go away to prep school, Arthur Moore enjoyed the advantages and the self-confidence of the eldest son in a wealthy family of devout Anglican Christians, with a strong sense of responsibility as paternalistic employers and leading figures in Manx public life. He already had a powerful attachment to his family, to their home at Cronkbourne, and to the Island of his birth.

A. W. Moore's paternal grandparents James (1772-1846) and Elizabeth (*née* Jeale) Moore (1775-1845). James bought the estate of Ballafletcher in 1825, and built the fine new mansion of Cronkbourne. Later in the century the family's architect cousins Henry and Ewan Christian both made alterations and extensions to the building. This view of the west (entrance) front was taken in about 1900.

A contemporary portrait of Arthur's grandfather James Moore, still in the possession of the family.

A late nineteenth century photograph of part of Cronkbourne Village, built by the Moore family for the workers at their sailcloth factory.

A. W. Moore's father William Fine Moore (1814-95) and mother Hannah (*née* Christian, 1827-1914). John Quine, who often took a jaundiced view of life, described her as 'a socially clever pitiless merciless mother'.

Arthur William Moore (born in 1853), at the age of three or four; it was during this period that he was terrorised by a sadistic nursemaid.

Arthur in 1865, aged twelve and about to go away to prep school in Weybridge. He was unhappy there because of bullying by both boys and masters, but greatly enjoyed Rugby School, where he started in 1867.

Chapter 2

EDUCATION

The earliest reference to Arthur Moore's education tells us that in 1861, at the age of eight, he was receiving Latin lessons from the Revd Robert Airey, then the chaplain of St Luke's Chapel, Baldwin, who lived conveniently close to home at Bridgemount Cottage, Tromode.[1] For the next few years he was educated at private schools in Douglas, and also by a private tutor. The first of these, in 1862, was the Atholl Academy at the Crescent, headed by Isaiah McBurney LLD. Moore recalled going there on a pony, and M. Victor Pleignier, the French teacher whose main employment was at King William's College, throwing books at his head.[2] Nevertheless, he received three school prizes at the midsummer ceremony from Samuel Harris, High Bailiff of Douglas. For the next two years he moved to another school run by a Mr Shaw, a retired naval officer. He also, in the summer of 1865, received private tuition from Philip Elliott, a twenty-two year old Cambridge graduate, son of a surgeon, also Philip, and his wife Eleanor, a devout and indefatigable charitable worker amongst the poor of Douglas.[3]

These fragments of information do not add up to very much. Until he was twelve, Arthur's schooling took place against the secure background of family life at Cronkbourne, but all that changed when he left home for the first time to attend Weybridge School, a preparatory school in Surrey. John Quine's notes record laconically, 'Dr Spiers severe. Bullied by masters and boys'. Moore may have been the victim of bullying between the ages of twelve and fourteen because of his short stature, or because he came from a remote island in the Irish Sea of which his tormentors had never heard; at this age boys are often at their worst, and bullies focus on anyone who is different in any way. Bullying by masters as well would have been an extra burden to bear. However he responded, Arthur must have found Weybridge School a traumatic experience. It is probably no coincidence that during this period he was 'ill with erysipelas and generally', and that at the age of fourteen he was considered a delicate boy.

There were consolations. Like many isolated children, Arthur was a keen reader and eagerly devoured Macaulay's *History of England* and the novels of Sir Walter Scott. He also spent the Easter holidays getting to know some of his English relations, staying in 1866 with a Willy Moore and his wife at East Molesey in Surrey, and in Harley Street with his uncle by marriage, John Loughborough Pearson, in 1867.

John Pearson was renowned as a leading church architect and restorer in the Victorian neo-Gothic style. His mother, Nancy Loughborough (1776-1869), was a Manxwoman, and in 1862 he had married Arthur's aunt, Jemima Christian. Jemima died of typhoid fever only three years later. Their only son Frank (1864-1947), who was eventually to join his father's architectural practice, was a frequent visitor to Cronkbourne with an unmarried aunt, Sarah Christian, and may in fact have been largely brought up there. Despite the eleven-year age difference between them, he and his cousin Arthur became lifelong friends.[4]

Among other London relations were Uncle Henry Christian (1831-1906), whose architectural practice was London-based but who designed Braddan School in 1858, the Ballamona Lunatic Asylum in 1864, and Bride Church in 1872, and his older cousin Ewan Christian (1814-1895), also London-based but responsible for St Thomas's Church, Douglas (1847), and other churches in Marown, Laxey and Ballasalla. Both men at different times worked on alterations and extensions at Cronkbourne.[5]

Like his father before him, Arthur Moore had his horizons widened and his life enriched by close contact with his mother's London relatives, who constituted an extraordinary network of Anglo-Manx church architects and their families. He remained close to most of these relations throughout their, and his, lives. More immediately, from fourteen on, he was never short of a place to stay in London, and a base from which to explore the capital.

In the summer holidays of 1867 Arthur was coached for the entrance exams at Rugby School by the Vicar of Braddan's younger son Thomas Wortley Drury, then still a Cambridge undergraduate, later to become the first Manx Bishop of Sodor and Man in modern times (1907-11). The tuition Thomas Drury gave him was good enough for Moore to attain the last place but one in the middle school.[6]

As John Quine said in his memoir, 'The Rugby period, 1867-72, after a somewhat dismal experience of preparatory schools, was to him a new and wholly congenial life'. Attending a great public school, with all its traditions, hierarchy and regulations, arcane customs and vocabulary, appealed to Arthur Moore enormously. And Rugby, ever since the reforms instigated by the famous Dr Thomas Arnold, headmaster from 1828 to 1842, was a school ruled not by bullying but by moral earnestness. Moore's memories of his time there focused heavily on sporting activity. In his first year he played football and fives, rowed, took part in paper chases and 'house-washing', which meant leaping across the River Avon as far as possible until, as the river widened downstream, finally one fell in. He ran the mile in five minutes, eleven seconds. As a result of pushing himself hard, he ended up in the school infirmary with inflammation of the lungs. Later in his school career he suffered from measles, then bronchitis.

He played Rugby football, the school's original contribution to sport, throughout his schooldays, graduating from the second to the first House Twenty, and then into the School Twenty (at that time a Rugby team consisted of twenty men, not fifteen as now). But the activity he enjoyed most, and in which his prowess was recorded in the school magazine, *The Meteor*, was rifle shooting and the school corps, which he joined in his first term. He won several shooting prizes, went to summer camps and battalion drills in various places in the Midlands, and by the time he left school had attained the rank of Colour Sergeant in the corps. He was in the Rugby team shooting in the Public Schools Competition at Wimbledon. This activity spilled over into the summer holidays of 1871, when Moore and his Island friend George Drinkwater, a pupil at Eton, challenged any two of the Manx Volunteers to a shooting contest, and won. As Quine says, 'At Rugby [Moore] devoted himself to games – not with the simple enthusiasm of the athlete, but with a singular earnestness and conviction with regard to their value ... and he achieved distinction as an athlete far beyond the warrant of his physical fitness'. This 'muscular Christianity' was an important part of the Rugby School ethos.

Academically, Moore's level of achievement fluctuated. In the spring term of 1868 he came top and won the form prize, but on being moved into a higher class he came bottom in the term's work, though he did better in the exams. He wrote an essay on Scandinavian history, of which he knew little, but he mentioned the Manx crosses, and as a result was given top marks by the Revd R. C. E. Moberley, who liked originality. In the Easter term of 1869 he became ill again, did no work and returned to the bottom of the form. This must have spurred him on to make a great improvement and carry off prizes in English, history and geography at the end of the year. Although there are no prize inscriptions in the books, these could perhaps have been the twelve-volume set of J. A. Froude's *History of England from the Fall of Cardinal Wolsey to the Defeat of the Spanish Armada* (1870), which is still in the possession of the Moore family. In the Fifth Form (1869-71) he got his own study to work in for the first time, but by 1871 he again had a poor school record. In his last year, in the Sixth Form, he studied not much classics, but chemistry and political economy. There are a few signs of wider interests emerging: in the autumn of 1871 he attended the Debating Society and voted against the conduct of the House of Lords during the previous session, against the then (Conservative) government's policy on Ireland, and against women's suffrage (with the majority of nineteen to six). He also acted the part of Dangle in an extract from Sheridan's play *The Critic*. In the summer of 1872 he went to Trinity College, Cambridge, and passed his Matriculation – i.e. was awarded a place – probably after a determined bout of last-minute swotting. In later life he believed that with better teaching between the ages of ten and fourteen he could have got an Exhibition, but that at that time he had 'got no real scholarship'.[7]

Moore's time at Rugby was worthy but not particularly distinguished. As with most boys, Rugby made a greater impact on him than he did on Rugby. He enjoyed the camaraderie of school life, and later on in life was always pleased to meet Old Rugbeians. By present-day standards the school might be seen as providing a very conventional education, but that is a misleading perspective. In fact Rugby was the most liberal and academically successful of the great English public schools, by the standards of the day – perhaps even in the Moore family – too liberal. A conversation at home at Christmas 1869 produced an 'argument against going [to Rugby] as "so broad" and "such a radical place"', according to Quine's notes, though who expressed these views is not known; possibly Arthur's Uncle Joseph, the Archdeacon.

The Head of Rugby from 1857 to 1869 was Frederick Temple (1821-1902), an educational and social reformer as well as a clergyman who thought that living a Christian life was more important than argument about the theological niceties of Anglican doctrine. At Rugby he enlarged and systematised the teaching of history, made English language and literature compulsory subjects, and introduced science, music and drawing into the curriculum. Moore's schooling benefited from these reforms. He was sixteen when Temple left to become Bishop of Exeter, and he remembered only one encounter. He asked to leave a day early at the end of term, on account of the distance he had to travel to get home to the Isle of Man. Temple replied, 'Oh, why do you live in such an outlandish place? You may go!!' Nevertheless Moore called on Temple when he was in Exeter in 1873; his old headmaster later became Archbishop of Canterbury (1896-1902). Moore shared the general view of his controversial successor as Head, Dr Henry Hayman, whom he considered 'hopeless', and a poor disciplinarian.[8]

A teacher at Rugby who became a lifelong friend was his housemaster, James Wilson (1836-1931), who taught maths and science. Wilson had been born and brought up in the Isle of Man, the son of the first Principal of King William's College, where he was educated. In 1868 he married a

Manxwoman, Annie Moore, a cousin of Arthur's, whom he met whilst staying at Cronkbourne. Later in life Wilson too was ordained and became Headmaster of Clifton College, where he was a friend of T. E. Brown.[9]

Moore's house tutor – a kind of personal counsellor and junior house-master – was Arthur Sidgwick (1840-1920), a classical scholar educated at both Rugby and Trinity, who taught classics, English, history and divinity; also political economy at the top of the school. He must have encouraged and assisted Moore to gain entrance to Trinity, where he himself held a Fellowship (1864-9) at the same time as teaching at Rugby. Sidgwick was a progressive liberal and university reformer, opposed to Church of England religious tests. Well-connected in the Church of England and at Cambridge, he was the brother of the philosopher Henry Sidgwick, and definitely part of the 'intellectual aristocracy'.[10]

Moore made a large number of friends and acquaintances during his time at Rugby, an 'old boy network' many of whom he would meet again in later life. But his teachers were particularly influential. They introduced him to a public school ethos which combined extrovert muscular Christianity with a respect for learning, good works and practical liberalism. These values would sustain and guide him throughout his life.

Various activities in the school holidays also contributed to the enlargement of his experience. At Easter 1869 he again stayed with the Pearsons in Harley Street, and began a long habit of London theatre-going. He saw *Caste* (1867) and *School* (1869), both plays characterised by a new domestic realism, the so-called 'cup-and-saucer drama' of their newly-fashionable author T. W. Robertson; the playwright's innovations would later be described by George Bernard Shaw as 'a theatrical revolution'.

When in camp at Wimbledon in 1871 Arthur met his uncle Henry Christian, there in the Artists' Corps of Volunteers, and was taken by him to the tent of Frederick (later Lord) Leighton, the painter and sculptor, where they all enjoyed drinking champagne from a silver cup. In February 1872 he was one of fifteen boys from Rugby, Eton and Harrow who had tickets for the Thanksgiving Service held at St Paul's Cathedral to celebrate the recovery of the Prince of Wales from serious illness. He saw Disraeli, Gladstone and the royal family, and was surprised at the small size of the queen. Arthur Moore was beginning to show a marked taste for the company of the rich and famous, and a strong admiration for aristocracy and monarchy, very much in line with the conventions of his social milieu.

Holidays, too, became more adventurous. In 1870 the Moore family visited the Lake District, and Arthur went on to Arkland, a moorland farm near Gatehouse of Fleet in Galloway, where he enjoyed his first experience of grouse-shooting. Back in the Lakes on the way home, he climbed Scafell Pike. The following year there was more grouse-shooting, as well as rabbits and 'black game', when Arthur stayed with the Faulder family at Roddam Hall in Northumberland, near Alnwick. A holiday in Norway in August 1872 with a small party of masters and boys was a kind of farewell to his schooldays. The party included James Wilson, Arthur Sidgwick, two other boys, Charles Wilson (the housemaster's younger brother, a Cambridge undergraduate), and Graham Dakyns, T. E. Brown's friend and colleague on the staff of Clifton College, with his brother. They 'roughed it' in the mountains and fjords around Stavanger and Bergen for a few weeks, carrying knapsacks, presumably camping and walking, and living off the equivalent of half-a-crown (two shillings and sixpence) a day. On the way home, Moore visited Lincoln Cathedral, which his uncle John Pearson was in the process of restoring.

The network of Anglican public schoolmasters with Manx connections was a striking feature of Moore's social world. Arthur Sidgwick was probably the most influential of his teachers. At the end of Moore's schooldays, Sidgwick taught him Political Economy, and it is very likely that the annotated copy of John Stuart Mill's *Considerations on Representative Government*, (signed A. W. Moore, 1872, and still in the possession of his family) dates from this time. Not only was Sidgwick on the Norwegian expedition in the summer of 1872, but he and Charles Wilson also came to stay at Cronkbourne in the Easter holidays of 1873. The three young men (Sidgwick was still only thirty-three) had a picnic on the Calf and bathed in the dangerous waters of the Sound. Sidgwick had homosexual proclivities, was a friend of John Addington Symonds, and in 1866 had enjoyed what was at least a passionately emotional relationship with a boy at Rugby. His tendencies may have enhanced his appreciation of Arthur Moore's company, but there is no reason to suppose that things went any further than that. Moore showed no inclinations in that direction, and given his conscientious, dutiful character he would almost certainly have resisted any sexual approach. Later in 1873 Arthur Sidgwick married James Wilson's sister Charlotte, with whom he had five children.[11]

Life at Trinity College, Cambridge, was described by Moore as characterised by an 'immense sense of freedom' after Rugby. Seven or eight Rugby boys 'stuck very much together'. They enjoyed swimming, cards and football. Moore joined the Boat Club and rowed in the freshmen's trial eight; he had rooms in college, rather than lodgings, in the summer term. He struck up a friendship with a 'recluse' called Hellyer who spent his time reading Herbert Spencer and playing the piano, tennis and chess, in the last of which Moore joined him (Hellyer later went into the diplomatic service, and died in 1895). Another new friend, Le Breton, from Jersey via Radley College, was an enthusiast for modern dance music.

Apparently Moore, like many undergraduates, did little work in his first year. Indeed he told Quine that 'Neither AWM nor any Rugby man did any work whatever!' It remains unclear precisely what course of study he was following: there are references to maths lectures ('Euclid unfamiliar'), to German, and to the eighteenth century philosopher and theologian, William Paley. Moore joined the college's Magpie and Stump debating society and spoke in favour of the proposition that corporal punishment should be more generally inflicted on criminals (carried by ten votes to four) – a point of view he is unlikely to have supported in later life.[12] But all this seems to have been of secondary importance. The summer term was delightful, devoted to rowing, canoeing and watching, but not playing, cricket. Moore also kept a collie dog in the college.

Home for the long vacation in 1873, he enjoyed the first trip on the Isle of Man Steam Railway from Douglas to Peel on 1st July, with the locomotive being driven by the Duke of Sutherland, one of the main investors, and a celebratory banquet in an engine shed to follow. In August and September he undertook a month's energetic walking tour in the West Country with a friend called Paul who lived at Tetbury in the Cotswolds. They walked in Gloucestershire, Devon and Cornwall, where they took a boat trip from Penzance to the Scillies, explored Land's End and the Lizard, and caught a train from Falmouth to Bodmin before striking north to Tintagel and the North Devon coast. This arduous month in the open air occupied thirty-eight pages of the missing travel diaries.

Arthur Moore's second year at Cambridge (1873-4) was more serious-minded, and his energies became more focused. He did not abandon sport, and rowed in inter-college races, but he also began to read for the Historical Tripos. He entered Cambridge in a period of reform, although the account of his first year might not suggest it. There was a tradition that most wealthy or aristocratic undergraduates tended to congregate in Trinity. But things were changing, and after the 1860s a Cambridge college was 'no longer mainly a romantic retreat, but a place where the teacher influenced the student by example, knowledge or sympathy'. One of the important signs of change was the appointment of John Seeley as Regius Professor of History in 1869, and the reforms which followed. Seeley established the study of history at Cambridge in its own right and not, as earlier, a subsidiary part of a degree in Moral Sciences or law. Although originally a classicist, Seeley was convinced of the importance of history in educating politicians and statesmen. 'Patriotism should be inculcated, national history closely connected with morality, and civil duties carefully explained'. Seeley later wrote the classic statement of an imperialist historical outlook, *The Expansion of England* (1883). This approach to what was in effect a new university subject – like sociology a century later in the 1960s – was challenging, but compatible with the Rugby ethos with which Moore was familiar.

Seeley's approach was not universally welcomed at Cambridge. His predecessor, Charles Kingsley, was a man better known, now as then, for his literary rather than historical abilities, as a novelist and the author of such popular Victorian children's classics as *Westward Ho!* (1855), *The Water Babies* (1863), and *Hereward the Wake* (1865). After listening to Seeley's inaugural lecture in 1870, entitled 'The Teaching of Politics', in which he emphasised the power of history, as 'the school of statesmanship', to illuminate the present and the future, the classics don Henry Montagu Butler, headmaster of Harrow and later Master of Trinity, said 'Dear, dear, who would have thought that we should so soon have been regretting poor Kingsley?' His remark has since been described, by G. R. Elton, as 'the finest double anti-compliment ever uttered'. But Seeley (1834-95, knighted in 1894) achieved the emancipation of history at Cambridge from the dilettante approach exemplified by Kingsley.[13]

Arthur Moore was among the first cohort of undergraduates to read for the new Modern History tripos, and attended the lectures of Seeley and Basil Hammond, a Trinity College tutor who was another product of Rugby. Whether through working too hard or rowing too hard, Moore had another bout of bronchitis and spent the Easter holidays of 1874 in Ventnor, Isle of Wight, where he convalesced.

But in the summer term he both returned to rowing in one of the college boats, and won first class marks and a prize in the college exam on his tripos subject. He chose a twelve-volume set of the novels of William Makepeace Thackeray (1811-63), the author of *Vanity Fair* and also a former undergraduate for two years at Trinity, 'where he fell in with a fast set and lost heavily at cards, leaving in 1830 without taking a degree'.[14] Moore was a loyal college man, and may have chosen the works of Thackeray simply because he had been at Trinity.

In the long vacation of 1874, Moore spent six weeks travelling in the far north of Scotland, initially with Ball, a college friend, as far as the Orkneys. When Ball was summoned home by his family, Moore fell in with a canoeist called Armstrong, with whom, according to Quine, he embarked on a very dangerous adventure. Quine's tantalizingly brief notes on the travel diaries, which for the most part contain only the bare facts of Moore's itineraries, say simply 'Canoeist Armstrong – Scapa Flow – Kirkwall. Sat 18 July sail in canoe Dunnet Bay [which is adjacent to the Scottish mainland]'. Another set of notes, based partly on conversations with Moore, says 'Armstrong with Canoe. Crossed Pentland Firth', which is also ambiguous. Quine's published account, in the preface to *Nessy Heywood*, is more expansive: 'At Stromness he found a stranger named Armstrong, who had crossed the Pentland Firth in a canoe; and now invited him to join him on the passage back. It was a risky adventure. The canoe was caught in a squall in the Race of Pentland; and his career, then and there, at the age of 21, all but ended'. The Pentland Firth is one of the most dangerous stretches of water in the British Isles. If Moore and Armstrong really did cross it in a canoe, this was a remarkable feat of youthful daredevilry, its success owing more to luck than judgement. The pair caught a train to Inverness and travelled to the west of Scotland via the Caledonian Canal and Loch Ness, before they parted company and Moore returned to the Island and Cronkbourne.

In his third year at Cambridge, he gave up rowing and concentrated on Rugby football, getting into the university team and winning his Blue. But above all, he concentrated on hard work for his tripos exams or finals, which in those days took place in October, after the completion of the university year. During this period of intensive work, little else occurred which was worthy of record. He again won first class marks in the college history exam at the end of the summer term, this time choosing as his prize an eight-volume set of Charles Knight's *Popular History of England* (1856) – which has not turned out to be an enduring classic. He took a shorter holiday break than usual in July, visiting Edinburgh, the Trossachs and the Scottish Lakes – Loch Katrine and Loch Lomond.

In the October term, Moore was still playing football in the Varsity team, but withdrew from the match against Oxford at the Oval because it occurred the day before his exams started. He now faced the culmination of all his academic efforts, and took eight papers: Outlines of English History, plus three special subjects (on these four papers the questions were almost entirely factual rather than interpretative), together with Political Philosophy and Jurisprudence, Constitutional Law, Political Economy and Economic History, and International Law.[15] The imprint of the approach to history embodied in this course of study can still be discerned in Moore's masterwork, *A History of the Isle of Man*, published twenty-five years later.

For the present, Moore was an industrious student whose conscientious and well-organised approach to his subject paid off. In December 1875, when the results were announced, he had achieved the coveted First Class Honours. Inclined to be a competitive perfectionist, he later told John

Quine, himself an Oxford graduate, that he had not quite achieved the top First of his year 'through mistake in paper – took only one part of it'. His achievement would have been enough to satisfy most people. To the advantages of his upbringing and education he had now added both sporting and academic distinction, and he was equipped with the confidence and connections appropriate for a member of the Victorian upper-middle class elite, in the Isle of Man, England, and the wider world.

Arthur's parents William Fine Moore (standing, left, with umbrella) and Hannah (seated, centre, holding fan) at a Braddan parish bazaar held in the grounds of the Castle Mona in about 1882.

On his father's death, William Fine Moore had purchased Cronkbourne from the heir, his bachelor elder brother Joseph Christian Moore (1802-86), Rector of Andreas, who later became Archdeacon. Joseph was revered in the family, and as a young man Arthur Moore would walk all the way from Douglas to Andreas to visit him. In *Manx Worthies* he described his uncle as a 'man of deep personal piety... in social life he was truly hospitable, and very popular. His genuine wit and quaintness of speech were well known'.

A group with some of Arthur's siblings, including his young brother Godfrey, in costume for some kind of fête in 1878. His sisters' governess was a Miss Beale, but not the famous Dorothea, who was principal of Cheltenham Ladies College from 1858; she may have been a younger relative. Both Arthur's daughters would be sent to Cheltenham.

Arthur's youngest sister Katie Mildred (always known as Mildred in the family) did not marry, but after finishing school in Paris went on to a distinguished nursing career. She worked in Jerusalem, and as matron of the Red Cross Hospital in London went out to Serbia to help combat the 1915 typhus epidemic. In 1918 she was awarded the Royal Red Cross.

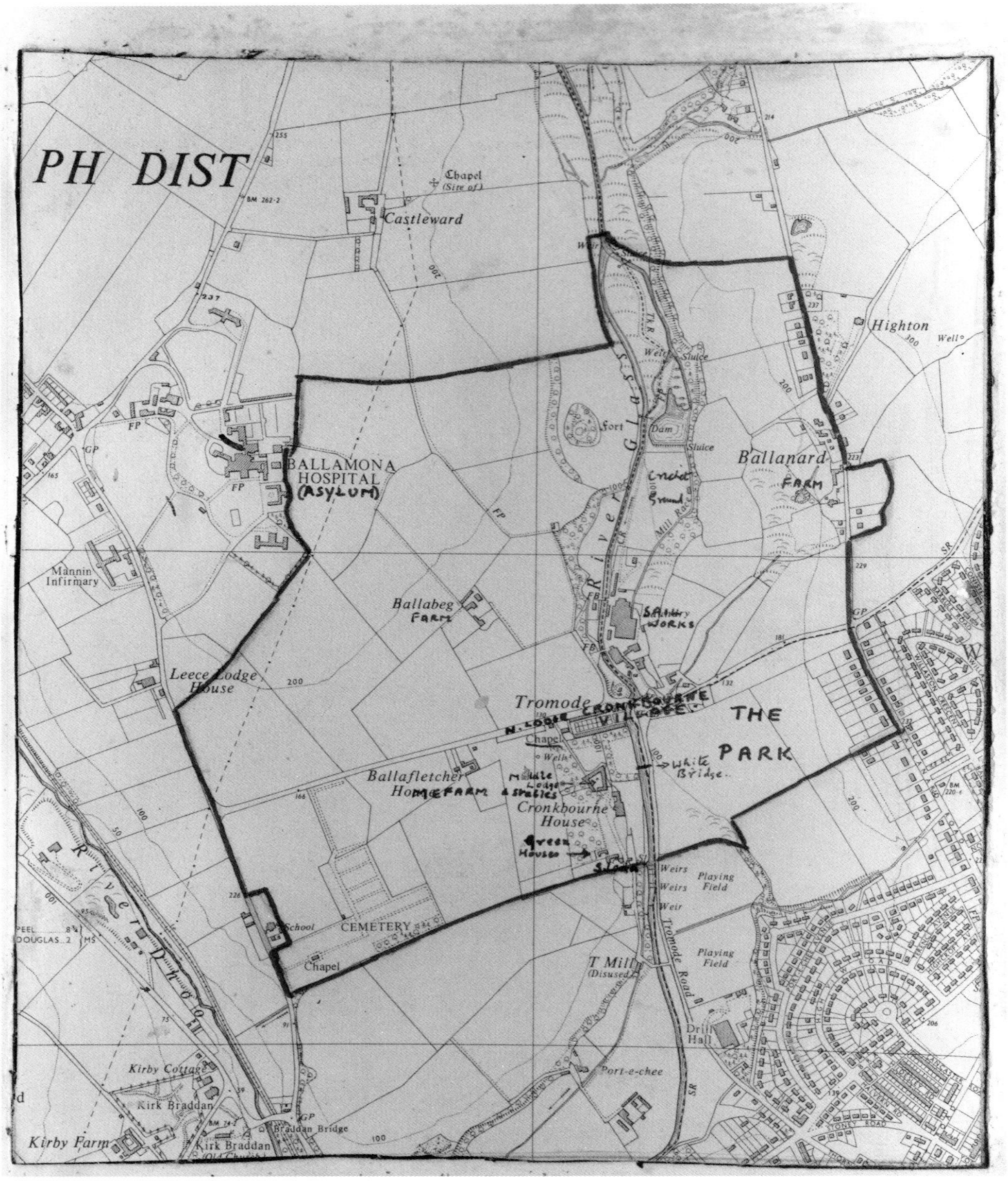

The limits of the Cronkbourne estate, outlined by a member of the Moore family on a mid-twentieth century map of Braddan.

Chapter 3

YOUNG MAN

According to his father, Arthur Moore, after achieving his first class degree, 'consequently had the offer of a very satisfying tutorship had he remained, but he elected to remain in the Isle of Man and help me'[1] – very much as William Fine Moore had chosen to help his own father and to return from London to the Island in 1831. At the age of sixty, W. F. Moore's health was declining, and in January 1875 he had resigned from the House of Keys. He badly needed his son's help with the family business.

But first Arthur deserved a reward for his degree and respite from his arduous intellectual labours. His father, after leaving school, had spent six months with relatives in London. Forty-five years later, the family fortunes had increased to the point where six months could be devoted to something like the Grand Tour enjoyed by the sons of the nobility in the eighteenth century. It was the first of a series of extensive journeys which Arthur Moore was to make during the next few years.

His first trip abroad began with an invitation to spend a month in the south of France with the family of W. B. Close, a Trinity College friend. After leaving Cambridge in mid-December 1875, he passed a few days with his parents in Brighton, crossed the Channel to Dieppe and travelled by train, via Paris (remarking on the snow south of Lyons), straight to the Riviera. Closebrooks, a villa with a garden by the sea, lay at the end of the Cap d'Antibes, four miles from Antibes railway station. During his stay with the Close family, Moore was entertained by other members of the colony of rich expatriates living on the Côte d'Azur. There was a Mrs Wyllie in the Villa Eileen Roc, and a Russian family called the Cazalets at the Villa des Colonnes, where there were entertainments, waxworks and theatricals; Arthur impersonated Napoleon I. The young man, affable, well-educated and with impeccable manners, was made thoroughly welcome. He spent a fortnight learning French at the Hôtel de France, Cannes, and was then invited to spend a further fortnight with a Mrs Richardson and her family at the Villa Mont Fleuri, also in Cannes.

In mid-February Moore set off with his friends Trevelyan and Duff for a ten-week tour of Italy; they travelled via Nice, Turin, Genoa and Pisa to Rome, where they stayed for the best part of a month (20 February-16 March). Before leaving England Moore had acquired a letter of introduction to Cardinal Giacomo Antonelli, who in turn gave him an order for a private audience with Pope Pius IX on 10 March. They conversed in both French and Italian, and the brief interview ended with a papal blessing, and the Pope expressing his hope that Moore would convert to Catholicism. In 1876 the Pope doubtless had a less crowded schedule than his more recent successors, but even so the episode shows remarkable social confidence and aplomb on the part of the twenty-three year old Moore. It may be worth repeating John Quine's comment on this episode: 'Though in later life he never acquired, probably never attempted to acquire, conversational facility as a fine art, he did acquire by the cultivation of social experiences an absolute freedom from that diffidence which men too commonly find an impediment in their interviews with their social superiors'.

His last month in Italy included further extensive travels, to Naples, Vesuvius, Pompeii, Amalfi, Sorrento and Capri in the south, then north again to Perugia, Siena and Florence, via Bologna to Venice, west via Verona and Milan to Lake Lugano, and back to Turin. The three friends arrived in Paris for a farewell dinner on 21 April at one of the city's most famous restaurants, Le Grand Véfour, before they parted. Moore then spent five weeks in Caen further improving his French, returned to London, dropped in at Cambridge to pick up his degree, and finally returned to the Isle of Man in early June.

He did not apparently find it hard to readjust to life in the Isle of Man, for he had never ceased to be attached to the Island. Throughout the years of his education he had sustained his interest in Manx affairs, private and public, whether the births, marriages and deaths of friends and acquaintances or the actions and decisions of Tynwald and ceremonial occasions. Through his father, he knew most of the members of the House of Keys, the Governor, the Bishop and other leading citizens.

He got straight down to work as his father's clerk, picking up the details and routine of the sailmaking business, according to Quine, 'with a rapidity rather surprising to the factory staff'. He spent ten days in June in Northern Ireland in order to learn the ropes of flax-buying, staying with Robert Boyd near Armagh and visiting the flax markets at Ballibay, Monaghan and Colehill. He then moved on to stay with a Major Blackley, to acquaint himself with the work of the branch factory at Monkstown near Belfast. Back in the Island, he took the lead in establishing the Cronkbourne Cricket Club as a healthy outdoor activity for the men and boys at the works, setting an example by teaching himself how to play. Naively, at best, he complained that the workers were 'lazy' and needed physical exercise.

Arthur Moore was a young man in a hurry. In October 1876, aged only twenty-three, he was appointed as a JP. But his appointment was not made public until the following March, when the announcement was greeted with surprise and vociferous objections by the editors of two leading Manx newspapers. 'Who is Arthur Moore?', asked the editor of the *Isle of Man Times*, and answered his own question, 'A mere stripling from the University. He has figured as a reader before the intellectual audiences which usually assemble at the penny readings held at Cronkbourne and at the Lunatic Asylum'. The appointment was a blatant case of 'family favouritism'. The *Times* returned to the attack the following week, referring to 'public indignation and widespread dissatisfaction' at this 'indefensible' appointment. Moore was too young, inexperienced, ignorant of the law and the courts. The *Mona's Herald* joined in, claiming that Moore could only have obtained the honour 'as a compliment to his excellent father'.[2] Young Mr Moore was an amiable, excellent and cultured gentleman, but amiability, intelligence and education alone were insufficient qualifications. After that, the row died down. As Moore himself recognised, he owed his elevation to the magistracy to the Governor's recommendation. Henry Brougham Loch, the Island's Governor from 1863 to 1882, was a highly effective reformer and moderniser. It was very unusual, even unprecedented, for a man of twenty-three to be appointed a magistrate, but in appointing Arthur Moore as a JP Loch knew what he was doing: he was recruiting an educated and talented young man to a career of public service in the Island. There were no subsequent complaints about Moore's conduct on the bench, and it was the only time in his career that he incurred public criticism.

The years between the mid-1870s and mid-1880s constitute a distinct phase of Arthur Moore's life. He was still unmarried, living in the bosom of his family at Cronkbourne until 1887. He had not yet published any books, though he founded and took on the editorship of the *Manx Note Book* in 1885. He entered the House of Keys in 1885. It may also be significant that he began to keep a diary in the same year; the entries dated earlier were a retrospective piecing together of information he wished to record, but about events which had happened some time before.

These bachelor years, however, were not entirely carefree. The ailing William Moore took his son into partnership in January 1877, when Arthur had only six or seven months' experience. In practice, Arthur Moore soon took on the main responsibility for running the family business, as his father became more or less an invalid for the remaining twenty years of his life.

In 1881 212 people lived in Cronkbourne Village, of whom about eighty were definitely employed at the works, and about the same number were children. Around fifty had been born in Ireland, an important source of skilled labour. W. F. Moore told the census enumerator that he employed 150 people, but this almost certainly included those who worked at the Monkstown factory in Ireland.[4] The workers at Tromode were still, presumably, subject to the list of thirty-nine rules and regulations which W. F. Moore had published in 1850. All his employees were expected to attend church at least once each Sunday; there was a sixty-eight hour, six-day, working week; and there was an elaborate list of punishments and fines for absence, lateness, neglect of work, damage to machinery, swearing, smoking, drinking and other misdemeanours.[5] To all appearances the firm of W. F. Moore & Son was strict but benevolent, according to the standards of the time, in its attitude to its workers, and enjoyed their loyal, not to say deferential, service. Housing was provided for them, along with a schoolroom and reading room. The enterprise became the largest private company in the Island, a model of industrial paternalism, and one of the few businesses 'to introduce a new flavour of industrialisation to the Isle of Man'.[6]

Since the company's books have not survived, we know very little about its record – a sad loss to the economic and social history of the Island. What difference, if any, did Arthur Moore make to the running of the firm? It is impossible to say. References to the business in his diary are few and far between, concerned mainly with visits to agents in London, Liverpool and Belfast. There is no reason to doubt that he carried out his duties conscientiously and that the firm remained successful until the market for sailcloth began to diminish, due to the prevalence of steamships. But the day-to-day running of the works was delegated to the mill manager, and presumably Moore recorded so little in his diary because he did not find it sufficiently interesting. Quine has probably got it right when he judges that Moore was not 'a born man of business, with the acquisitiveness that makes him in deadly earnest about acquiring a great fortune'. Had he been so, he might have sought to diversify the work of the firm away from sailcloth when demand decreased, 'but he did not have this incentive'.

The role of landed gentleman seems to have been more consistent with Moore's outlook and interests, and with the social status of an up-and-coming young member of the Anglo-Manx gentry. The Moore family had been substantial landowners since the 1820s, when they had bought the Ballafletcher estate which stretched well beyond the confines of Cronkbourne and Tromode (map, page 34). According to W. F. Moore, by 1830 the family interests included agriculture, and in 1851 he told the census enumerator that he farmed twenty acres. In the 1860s the Moores increased their landholdings considerably; in 1860 W. F. Moore bought Lanjaghan, an upland farm in the parish of Onchan, and in 1861 he bought the estate of Park Llewellyn near Ramsey for £2,700. According to James Woods' *Atlas & Gazetteer of the Isle of Man*, by 1867 he also owned about twenty-seven acres of land in Andreas. In 1873 Tromode Park, including over fifty acres, and a further thirty-four acres in Ballanard, were added to his holdings, at a cost of £4,800 and £2,460 respectively.

Arthur Moore's diary notes refer to a variety of agrarian, open-air and sporting activities. In 1877 he was involved in the foundation of a Hunt Club which took over a pack of harriers in the north of the Island, and he was secretary until its dissolution, due to lack of support, in 1883. He took to breeding fox terriers, and won prizes at the Douglas Dog Show in 1879. In 1881 he became President of the Isle of Man Agricultural Society, based in the south of the Island, and he was responsible for negotiating its amalgamation with the northern Manx Agricultural Society the following year. In 1882 he was elected President of the Island's Floral and Horticultural Society. He won prizes for breeding horses, poultry and bees, especially at the Castletown agricultural shows of 1885 and 1886. To misquote Gilbert and Sullivan, whose comic operas he much enjoyed, he was the very model of a modern country gentleman.

These activities were complemented by practical, hands-on involvement in farming, especially in the 1880s at Lanjaghan, which became a dairy farm with a herd of Ayrshire cattle and a Scottish herdsman to look after them – possibly John McTier, with whom Moore discussed the farm while passing through Dumfries in June 1882. From 1883 or 1884 on, cheese produced at Lanjaghan was on sale at several of the principal grocers' shops in Douglas, though after a few years the venture was abandoned because of competition from imported American cheese. In January 1886 Arthur Moore marked trees for felling in the upper plantation at Lanjaghan, and in September he spent several days cutting back vegetation round the edges of the fields, or supervising labourers who were doing it. He was kept especially busy during July and August. As he recorded in his diary on 4 July 1886: 'As Magee, the steward, has left, I now go up to Lanjaghan at night, sleep there, get the men to work at 6a.m. and then come down to breakfast at Cronkbourne. I utilise the pony for going to and fro, but it is hard work'. In November the farm was leased to a tenant.

Moore was also interested in sheep-rearing. He recorded with glee on 23 May 1885: 'Clip my sheep in the 'Park' a field of which I had rented – av. weight of wool 5 3/4lbs. per fleece'. On 14 May came unseasonal news: 'Hear that a number of our sheep and lambs on Slieau Loght mountain have perished in the snow'. For an active young man, livestock farming would seem a more attractive occupation than looking after the family business.

Arthur Moore was something of an all-round sportsman. His interest in shooting, begun at Rugby, continued for several years; his diary notes mention a shooting match between Cronkbourne and Douglas in October 1883. This interest was one he could share with the officers of the Royal Lancaster Volunteers and Royal Welsh Fusiliers, with whom he often fraternised during their summer camps in the Island. In 1879 the Fourth Battalion Lancashire Volunteers camped in Cronkbourne Park, and officers were entertained at a garden party at Cronkbourne attended by 150 people.

While still at Cambridge, Moore helped draw up the rules for the Island's Rugby Football Club, founded in 1873. But he devoted more time to cricket, although he had not played the game at Cambridge. In 1878 he was the captain of Douglas Cricket Club, but by the 1880s, if not before, he was playing for the Cronkbourne club which he had founded in 1876, and which was evidently a great success. He also enjoyed a game of tennis, usually at Kirby, the nearby home of his friends the Drinkwaters, or sometimes at Government House.

It was to be expected that an able and energetic young man of Moore's social standing would be co-opted into the public life of the Island and the official responsibilities of the governing elite. Following his appointment as a magistrate, he became involved in a variety of other activities. In 1878 he raised £50 to put Braddan Cemetery in order, was elected a member of the Braddan School Committee, and was admitted as a member of the Atholl Lodge of Freemasons, of which he became Worshipful Master in 1883. In 1880 he was a member of the first committee of the Douglas School of Art, art and architecture being among his interests, and in 1882 he spoke at the annual prizegiving ceremony at which the prizes were distributed by Lady Loch. In the same year he was appointed a Conservator of Fisheries under the Fresh Water Fisheries Act. In April 1885 he was elected as a Braddan churchwarden, and in December he became an honorary member of the Loyal Howard Lodge of Oddfellows.

Family duties were not neglected. The style of life at Cronkbourne seems to have reflected a rising standard of affluence. At the time of the 1881 census William and Hannah Moore and their seven resident children (four of whom, Arthur, Edith, Florence and Godfrey were for various reasons absent from home on census night) employed as living-in servants not only four females – cook, nurse, housemaid and kitchen-maid, all of Manx origin – but also two males, both from England, a butler aged thirty-one and a sixteen-year-old page. It was in keeping with the standards of this well-to-do household that Arthur, after visiting an Electrical Exhibition in London, should organise the installation of electric lighting at Cronkbourne in 1882.

Arthur Moore's antiquarian and historical interests were not yet widely known outside his own circle. He was, however, known for his interest in meteorology, which he was to sustain for forty years. In 1878 he started to keep weather records, set up his own observatory at Cronkbourne, and was given the official stamp of approval of the Meteorological Office in London, then based at Kew. In accordance with his usual practice of getting in touch with the leading person in any field that attracted his interest, in 1882 Professor John Knox Laughton, chairman of the Meteorological Society and head of the department of meteorology and marine surveying at Greenwich Naval College, was invited to lunch and inspected the Cronkbourne weather station.

Even in Arthur Moore's apparently charmed life there was an inescapable shadow of mortality. His father was well enough to travel by sea to Australia and back in 1884-5, but returned 'looking very ill'. The deaths of two infant brothers and the confinement of Harry in a lunatic asylum have already been mentioned. In December 1882 there was a further blow to the family when Arthur's sister Florence died, aged only twenty-two. He was moved, unusually, to add a couple of quotations to his diary notes. From the poet Longfellow:

To die?
And yet perhaps 'tis best
That she should die with all the sunshine on her
And all the benedictions of the morning,
Before this affluence of golden light
Shall fade into a cold and clouded gray,
Then into darkness!

And from the essayist Montaigne, reflecting on the day of death as the Day of Judgement.

Moore himself was not immune from accident and illness. In July 1882 he was returning from Lanjaghan with a friend named Beal, in a phaeton or light four-wheel carriage, when the horse bolted and galloped half a mile before dropping dead. Beal was thrown into a gorse hedge while Moore fell on top of the dying pony, was kicked on his head and body, and suffered a severe blow in the groin from the carriage step. Both men managed to walk home (it was the day Professor Laughton came to lunch), but there were repercussions. In December 1883 Moore became ill with 'congestion of the lungs and liver', and then the following January with acute pain in his left thigh, due to blocked veins from the old injury. He was confined to bed, suffering greatly, and recovered only in February. The condition returned again in December 1885 when he gave his left leg a bad strain.

Moore's zest for living was most apparent in the extraordinary range and variety of his holidays. He revisited Cannes and the French Riviera several times, in 1878 when he returned via Switzerland, in 1883 on his way home from Sicily, in 1884 when recovering from illness, and again in 1886. In the summer of 1877 he spent three weeks with Duff, one of his former travelling companions in Italy, at Hatton Castle, Aberdeenshire, his friend's family seat since the early eighteenth century and the centre of an estate of 12,000 acres. They also visited, and stayed with, other members of the Scottish landed gentry: Colonel Gordon at Fyvie Castle, Sir Robert Abercromby at Farglen, and Mr Urquhart at Meldrum Hall. This visit was repeated in 1885, when Moore opted out of his planned attendance at a conference of the British Association for the Advancement of Science in Aberdeen in favour of the pleasure of Duff's company at Hatton and 'social intercourse Dalgetty Castle etc.' He then proceeded south via Balmoral, Braemar and Perth as far as Edinburgh, where, with a return of scholarly conscientiousness, he spent two days copying rainfall data in the office of the Northern Lighthouse Board.

A holiday in Scotland in 1878 began with a voyage, from the Isle of Man to Arran and Oban, in the private yacht of Arthur Moore's London friends the Armitages. Edward Armitage (1817-96), professor of painting at the Royal Academy, and his wife Laurie (1818-98) were rich and successful artists who lived in St John's Wood. Arthur then stayed as a guest at Fairfield House, Ayrshire, home of a wealthy Glasgow tea merchant, and combined business with pleasure by returning via Ireland and staying with Captain Blackley, the man in charge of the branch factory at Monkstown. In all he visited Scotland five times during the years 1879-85, twice combining this with visits to Ireland.

His holiday in Sicily (February-April 1883), by ship from London to Naples, then Naples to Palermo, included a week's stay with the Whitaker family. Uncle Henry Christian was married to Caroline, daughter of Joseph Whitaker of Palermo, who had inherited from his uncle Benjamin Ingham vineyards, ships and a bank in Sicily. This wealthy family also owned several landed estates in England, and maintained their Sicilian possessions until the 1930s. Arthur's main friend in the family was one of Joseph's sons, Ingham Whitaker, but he also knew his brothers Arthur and Bob.[7]

Moore's holiday destinations included Belgium and northern France (a visit to the Louvre in Paris, and Chartres Cathedral), Bottisham Hall near Cambridge with his sisters to stay with the Campbell family, Yorkshire, and North Wales. In 1878 he captained the Douglas Cricket Club when they played matches in Ireland, at Rostrevor, County Down, and in Dublin's Phoenix Park; Moore went with two friends, Beal and Morris, to visit the Curragh Camp, County Kildare, Irish headquarters of the British Army.

Arthur Moore was an indefatigable tourist, who took every possible opportunity to travel and made good use of his connections, his social skills and his popularity as a guest. Yet his two longest journeys, lasting four and five months respectively, may be classified by their length and difficulty as travel rather than tourism. In January 1880, after another bout of bronchitis, he set off to visit Egypt and Palestine in the company of a Cambridge friend, Williams; they travelled on board the SS *Kedar* via Cape Finisterre (where the ship rolled alarmingly by thirty-two degrees), Gibraltar and Malaga. They visited Algiers and Malta en route to the port of Alexandria, then went on by rail to Cairo. After inspecting the Pyramids, they travelled up the Nile to Luxor, visiting the Valley of the Kings and other archaeological sites. Back in Cairo, Moore characteristically had lunch with Major Evelyn Baring (later Sir Evelyn, then 1st Earl of Cromer), who was British Consul-General in Egypt and in effect the man running the country. The two friends then took a Russian steamship from Alexandria to Port Said and Jaffa, and spent nearly a month in Palestine – then usually referred to as the Holy Land – visiting Jerusalem, Bethlehem, the Dead Sea, Jericho, the Sea of Galilee and many other biblical sites. For a devout Christian like Moore, this was a journey with religious as well as aesthetic and architectural significance. On his return to the Island he was in demand as a speaker on his travels, and as late as 1907 he gave a lecture on Jerusalem, illustrated with lantern slides.[8] Travelling north through the Levantine provinces of the decaying Ottoman Empire, in what are now Lebanon and Syria, he and Williams visited Tyre and Sidon, Beirut and Damascus, before taking ship for Cyprus, calling at Rhodes and other Greek islands, Smyrna on the Turkish mainland, and on to Constantinople. A French steamship conveyed them to Athens; they took another boat from Corinth to Corfu and north up the Adriatic to Trieste. A rail journey to Vienna, Munich, Nuremburg, through the Rhine valley to Cologne, Berlin, Hamburg, and a boat back to London completed this epic journey, surely exhausting even for a man of twenty-seven.

Nothing daunted, Moore set off across the Atlantic, as far as we know alone, in the SS *Medusa* from Southampton on 17 January 1881. The ship touched at the Azores before heading for the West Indies, sailing via Barbados, Trinidad and Tobago, Grenada, St Vincent, St Lucia, Martinique, Dominica, Guadalupe, Antigua, St Kitts, St Thomas, Puerto Rico, Santo Domingo and finally to Havana – having travelled around the outer arc of all the main Caribbean islands except Jamaica. A second ship took him to Vera Cruz, where he disembarked for the overland journey to Mexico City. Returning to Vera Cruz, he sailed up the Caribbean coast to New Orleans, where he stayed for a month, his first port of call in the USA. On 12 April he boarded the famous steamboat the SS *Robert E. Lee*, which took him up the Mississippi as far as Natchez, where he stayed with the Minor family. Another boat took him even further upriver, to L'Argent Landing, where he stayed with a Mr Izhaga and visited the cotton plantations. Eventually he went all the way via Memphis, Tennessee, to St Louis.[9]

He travelled on by rail to Chicago, then a city of stockyards and slaughterhouses, where on 30 April he witnessed a pig killing. Now he turned west across the plains of Wisconsin and Iowa, through Dubuque and the small town of Le Mars, to Sioux City on the Missouri River, returning to Chicago via Omaha (Nebraska) and Cedar Rapids. This journey west must have been undertaken in order to see his friend W. B. Close, who with his brothers had started a bank in 1878 and bought over 14,000 acres of fertile farmland in the prairies of Iowa. Moore was taken for an eight-mile drive around 'our farms'. The partnership had an office in Sioux City.[10] Next, a journey to Detroit, Niagara (into Canada) and Toronto, where he took a steamer via Lake Ontario and the St Lawrence River to Montreal, then another one to Quebec. After turning back to Montreal he headed south, crossed back into the USA, and then travelled by rail from Lake Champlain via Saratoga and Albany to New York. He made a round trip to Washington DC, then back to New York via Philadelphia. Next he went on to Boston, the battle-field of Bunker Hill, adjacent Cambridge (Massachusetts) and Harvard University, where he was introduced to the captain of the rowing eight and had lunch with the crew training for the boat race with Yale. For once giving us something more than an itinerary, Quine tells us that Moore was 'received almost with reverence as a Trinity, Cambridge man'. He visited the fashionable resort of Newport, Rhode Island, and took ship back to New York where he dined at the exclusive Knickerbocker Club, visited Staten Island (unfortunately five years too early to see the Statue of Liberty) and finally embarked for Liverpool, an eight-day passage. He arrived home at Cronkbourne on 7 June.

These itineraries are a poor substitute for the fuller accounts in Moore's missing travel diaries (ninety pages devoted to Egypt and Palestine, eighty-five to the Caribbean and North American journey, Quine tells us). But even to trace these journeys in an atlas and in imagination gives a better idea of the young Arthur Moore. As he approached thirty, his experience of life was no longer confined to the Isle of Man, public school and university, and the polite circles, including expatriates, of English high society. Meeting Arabs, West Indians and Mexicans, American farmers and riverboat crews had considerably broadened his experience of his fellow men.

The account in Moore's recently-commenced diary of his stay in London, 27 May-9 June 1885 (London being too familiar to be counted as 'travel'), gives a closer view of his social and cultural world. Arriving in the capital on 27 May, he stayed at 15 Mansfield Street, with his mother and sister Edith next door at number thirteen, home of John Pearson. The next day he called on his firm's London agents, lunched with the Armitages at their home, and went for a drive in Hyde Park. On 29 May he lunched in the City with W. B. Close, who was staying with his wife at Hampton Court. He visited 'The Inventories', a technical exhibition to which he returned twice – gas engines and electric lighting are mentioned. And, because the thermometer stood at 30°C. 'as it is too hot for much exertion, I content myself ... with listening to the excellent Irish Constabulary band'.

On 30 May he visited the Royal Academy's summer show – 'good on the whole', and amongst the paintings noted especially 'The Sheep Stealer' by the Irish artist Briton Rivière, 'A Reading from Homer' by Sir Lawrence Alma Tadema, 'The Dog in the Manger' by William Holman Hunt ('the painting of the calves in it is admirable'), and 'a magnificent portrait' by Herbert Von Herkomer, of 'Miss Grant'. On 1 June the Grosvenor Gallery exhibition included some fine portraits by George Richmond, and another 'perfect little gem' by Alma Tadema, a portrait of Lady Loyd Lindsay. Turning from contemporary paintings to Old Masters, Moore enjoyed a morning at the National Gallery, preferring a newly-acquired Raphael ('very fine indeed') to a Van Dyck.

He visited the theatre five times in the first eight days of June. *Peril* was 'a vile adaptation of a French play with a vulgar woman, Mrs Langtry, taking the heroine's part'. *Olivia* at the Lyceum was 'a poor perversion of *The Vicar of Wakefield*, Ellen Terry being the only redeeming point. Irving's part – the old vicar - did not suit him'. *The Private Secretary* was 'a broad farce – amusing but overdone'. *The Mikado*, however, was 'very bright, pretty and absurd. Grossmith was marvellous, more like india rubber than ever. Barrington's Lord High Executioner was admirable'. Finally, *The Candidate* at the Criterion was 'the best piece I have seen, but Wyndham shouts too much'.

On 31 May, Trinity Sunday, Arthur Moore went with his mother and some female cousins to St Matthew's, Westminster, the church where his old Rugby friend, W. B. Trevelyan, a clergyman's son, was now the vicar himself. Trevelyan had accompanied Moore to Italy, but was certainly now not living in high style. 'After the service I lunched with T. and his five curates. They live together in quite a monastic and ascetic style. They all seem very earnest men and are doubtless doing excellent work in one of the poorest districts of Westminster'. In the afternoon Moore went to Kew Gardens with Frank Pearson and another friend from the world of church architects, W. D. Caröe (1857-1938), at this time articled to John Pearson.

On 4 June he visited John Drinkwater Lawe, who was staying near Horsham in Sussex (Appendix II, page 157). The following day he spent the morning at the Salisbury Club, and dined there with Frank Pearson. They met two Manx friends, Robert S. Stephen MHK and George Drinkwater, later in the evening. On 6 June Moore, Pearson and Caröe, with Williams, Moore's travelling companion in Palestine, went to a Coaching Club meet and admired some fine teams of black and brown horses.

The next day was perhaps the best of the trip. Arthur, Frank, William Caröe and his younger brother Fred went by train to Maidenhead, where they took a four-oar boat and rowed up the Thames to Cookham. They stopped at an island owned by friends of the Caröes, the Golds, a wealthy family who included the brothers-in-law of Walter and Arthur Gilbey, the famous wine and spirit merchants.[11] 'They are vulgar folk, but kind hearted. We sat down about 30 to lunch. The wine was excellent!' They did some more rowing through lovely scenery, called in again at Gold Island for tea, and caught the 6pm train back to town.

This was an idyllic day on the river, reminiscent of Jerome K. Jerome's *Three Men In A Boat* (1889), and full of the pleasures of male good fellowship. But were there any women, apart from relatives, in Arthur Moore's life? The records are silent on this subject. But that was soon to change; on 25 November 1885, at the Castletown Chrysanthemum Show, Arthur Moore set eyes on Louisa Hughes-Games for the first time.

Chapter 4

FAMILY MAN

Throughout Arthur Moore's childhood and youth, the most revered of his relatives outside the immediate family at Cronkbourne was his uncle Joseph Christian Moore, the Archdeacon, always referred to in Moore's diary simply as 'Uncle'. A man of deep personal piety and an evangelical churchman of strong views, he inspired awe and respect; as a young man Arthur frequently walked all the way to Andreas to visit him. On one occasion, possibly in June 1879, the old man forbade him to walk home on a Sunday, so instead he set out at three o'clock on Monday morning and arrived home in time for breakfast. But by the 1880s the Archdeacon's powers were waning. In February 1886 he suffered a third stroke; Arthur was present when his uncle died, aged eighty-three or four, in the rectory at Andreas on 26 February.

The Archdeacon's funeral on 3 March coincided with quite extraordinary weather conditions. On 1 March it went on snowing continuously for nearly the entire twenty-four hours. The next day the Island's roads were blocked by deep snowdrifts, making access by road from Douglas to Andreas completely impossible. The Moore family chartered a boat, the SS *Ellan Vannin*, to take them to Ramsey, leaving Douglas at 10pm in the teeth of a fierce north-easterly gale. But as the steamship was approaching Ramsey pier a heavy sea struck and landed her on a sandbank. As Moore's diary tells us, 'There she lay broadside to the waves and bumped about in a most tremendous way, water coming freely into the cabin until the tide went out. If we had been on rocks instead of sand, she must have gone to pieces'. The family were unable to get off the boat until 4am when, with an escort of sailors and stewards, they walked to the Mitre Hotel and only gained entry after hammering on the door for twenty minutes. After breakfast they resumed their journey in a waggonette to Andreas, making a detour via St Jude's to get through, and arrived in time for the funeral at one o'clock.

This was the worst snowstorm in the Island since 1847, and the drifts between the rectory and the church were six feet deep in places. The Moores stayed for several days, starting to clear the house, tearing up letters, and distributing books according to the Archdeacon's wishes. The storm had been a dramatic experience, and showed their devotion to family and determination to attend the funeral at all costs. But 'Uncle's' death was also to determine the future course of his nephew Arthur's life. The new Archdeacon was Dr Joshua Hughes-Games (1830-1904), who had been principal of King William's College since 1866. Although Arthur had caught sight of his daughter Louisa the previous November, he had not actually met her. At the end of April 1886, however, he found himself travelling to Andreas with Louisa and her mother in order to discuss the state of the rectory with the new Archdeacon. He confided to his diary that 'Miss L. H-G is a most perfectly charming and lovely girl'. He had to return to Andreas in mid-May for the sale of his uncle's furniture. On 22 June he lunched at King William's College with Dr Hughes-Games, and noted 'L.H.G. more lovely and charming than ever'.

In the summer, another family loss occurred with the death on 31 July of his kinsman, the Revd William Bell Christian of Milntown. It was a busy summer for Arthur Moore, who was working at Lanjaghan, carrying out his duties as an MHK, welcoming English antiquarians to the Island and doing some research of his own. But he had some days off, including a splendid walk with Frank Pearson on 15 September: 'By rail to Foxdale, then up past the old slate quarries to the summit of South Barrule ... we then went on to the top of Cronk-ny-arrey-Lhaa and had a grand walk along the top of the cliffs to Fleshwick – across to Colby station, from whence by rail to Port Soderick and home on foot'.

The annual week in London in October included a day at the Colonial and Indian Exhibition and going to see Henry Irving in *Faust* at the Lyceum ('Irving's grimaces and contortions are marvellous, but the whole piece – *Walpurgisnacht* in particular – savours strongly of pantomime. It is gorgeously put on the stage'). He also took a four-hour tour of Westminster Abbey, including sights not open to the general public such as the wax figures of monarchs, conducted by W. D. Caröe.

There is no further mention of 'Miss L. H-G' until 30 October. 'Saw Miss L. Hughes-Games from the Free Library window and walked after her. On catching her up we walked to Mrs Ring's' (Louisa's elder sister Helena). A few days later the two sisters came to lunch at Cronkbourne. On 25 November, screwing up his courage to the sticking point, Arthur 'went to Andreas on <u>most particular business</u>'. He was kept in suspense for a week until 2 December, when he 'went to Andreas and settled my business <u>most happily</u>. The day of the <u>*coup d'état*</u>'. He later explained to John Quine that this curious way of describing his engagement was a reference to the fact that on this day in 1851 Louis Napoleon had mounted the coup which installed him as Emperor of France!

Arthur Moore was delighted with his new fiancée. Although another great storm on 8-9 December culminated in the fall of the spire of Braddan New Church, he 'went to Andreas and had a very delightful day with L.' before doing anything about it. He also began to get to know his future in-laws, who were part of a large family of professional people, clergy, lawyers and teachers. Joshua Hughes-Games, an Oxford first class mathematics graduate, switched – like a good many clergy at that time – between education and the Church. He had been headmaster of the Liverpool Institute (1862-6) and Louisa, his second daughter, had been born in Liverpool in 1864. Until the age of fifty he had been Joshua Jones, but the whole family changed their surname in 1880 in order to qualify for a substantial inheritance. Arthur spent Christmas Day at Andreas, where 'We had a merry party at dinner. The H-G family certainly can eat!' Financially, as well as in other ways, the heir-apparent of Cronkbourne and partner in W. F. Moore & Son of Tromode was a good catch for Louisa and her family.[1]

Louisa and her mother busied themselves looking for a suitable home in which the young couple might start their married life, and by early January a new house had been approved which the builder had promised to have finished by the end of April. Arthur and Louisa's first home was not, as is often supposed, Woodbourne House, but 2 Woodburn Place, on the western side of what is now a stretch of Woodbourne Road, between Albany Road and Thorny Road. It would have been rented, like their next and main married home, Woodbourne House.[2] From Arthur's point of view, proximity to his beloved Cronkbourne – not much more than a mile away – would have been an advantage of both houses, and there would have been no reason to buy anything else because he could confidently expect to inherit Cronkbourne one day.

The engagement was a short one, less than three months. When the couple were married at Andreas on 22 February 1887 Louisa was twenty-two, and Arthur had just turned thirty-four. A large crowd collected outside the church; triumphal arches were erected at the rectory gate and the church entrance. Frank Pearson was best man, and Arthur's four sisters were among the six bridesmaids. The service at two o'clock was conducted by the Bishop and the Revd J. H. Hughes Games, one of Louisa's brothers, and afterwards there was a reception at the rectory. The list of 130 donors of wedding presents published in the *Isle of Man Times* included everyone from the Governor and the Bishop to the servants at Andreas and Cronkbourne, and the Cronkbourne workpeople. Among the Island's main newspapers, only the staunchly radical and nonconformist *Examiner* failed to carry a report of the wedding.[3]

The newly-married Mr and Mrs Moore were driven off to Douglas at four o'clock, where they spent the night, or rather two nights, to avoid a bad crossing, at the Castle Mona Hotel. The honeymoon, which lasted a full six weeks, was an opportunity for Arthur to show his wife his favourite places in France and Italy; they followed what was to him a familiar route through Cannes, Nice and Antibes to Pisa, Florence and Milan, before returning to Paris. Unfortunately Louisa's jewellery, about £60 worth of family heirlooms, was stolen from luggage that was sent back from Cannes.

They returned home to find that, despite the builder's promises, their new home was still not ready, so they had to go and stay at Cronkbourne. Gradually, they settled into married life. On 1 June Arthur was persuaded to shave off the beard he had had for nine years. 'I feel very queer and cold without it, but am more than consoled by L's joy'. Two servants, Rebecca Moore, cook, and Kate Kewley, were engaged and installed in the new house to get it ready, and at last on 26 June the Moores were able to move in. Arthur grumbled that it was 'by no means complete, but still it is habitable'.[4] On 4 July the couple held their first dinner party, which went off very well, with Professor John Rhys and the Revd Ernest Savage as their guests.

On 15 July Louisa went to Andreas for a change, the Jubilee proceedings and the hard work involved in getting into the house having proved too much for her; she was also in the early stages of pregnancy. She stayed in Andreas for ten days, with Arthur visiting at the weekend. In August her mother suffered concussion after being thrown out of a carriage, and she went back for another few days. In September the couple spent a week in the Scottish Lakes and Edinburgh, again familiar territory for Arthur. A dinner party in November was attended by Louisa's sister Helena and her husband the advocate, later Attorney General, George Ring, a Dr Black, and Mr and Mrs Hall Caine. Arthur had met Hall Caine the previous year, and the author now 'presented us with his new novel *The Deemster* in 3 vols'. Christmas was again spent at Andreas Rectory, with services morning and evening, and 'tremendous eating at the Rectory in the interval'.

The following year began with theatricals at Government House, visits by brothers and sisters from both families, and a break-in. In mid-January 'we found that a man had got into the house through the larder window ... and carried off some eatables together with a pair of my drawers and boots. He had collected the silver together and would doubtless have taken it if the servants' alarm had not gone off at 4.30am instead of 6.30. This probably frightened him and he decamped. The marks left by his fingers which were

A studio portrait of Arthur Moore aged about thirty, taken by Abel Lewis in Douglas. After wearing a beard for nine years he was persuaded by Louisa, within four months of their marriage, to shave it off. He wrote in his diary, 'I feel very queer and cold without it, but am more than consoled by L's joy'.

Louisa Elizabeth Wynn Hughes-Games (1864-1937). When he first met her Arthur Moore described Louisa as 'a most perfectly charming and lovely girl'.

Arthur and Louisa's daughters, Helena (1888-1969) and Margery (1889-1965). They were followed by William Arnold, born October 1893, and a second son, Arthur Hughes-Games Christian (1895-1972).

smeared with jam were found all over the lower rooms'. A few days later 'My boots were discovered in a stack near Willaston and the same night the man was caught there with my drawers on him'. The burglar, William Griffiths, a 'notorious character' with a record of previous convictions who was sleeping rough, refused to admit his guilt. Described as 'a middle-aged man of miserable appearance', he was committed for trial at the High Court and sentenced to five years' penal servitude.[5]

On 24 February, almost exactly a year after the wedding, the Moores' first child, a daughter, was born without mishap – although a fortnight earlier Louisa had fallen downstairs going to her bath. The aftermath was difficult, with Louisa being feverish for several days, recovering, getting worse again in mid-March and then taking off with her mother and two nurses to Rushen Abbey Hotel, then to Port Erin. Arthur was not allowed to go near her. The baby was sent to Cronkbourne, and on 10 April privately christened Helena Christian Moore by her grandfather the Archdeacon in the drawing room. Louisa was 'somewhat better' by May, but on the 9th crossed with her mother to Ilkley in Yorkshire, 'where they stay at the Spa, L. being in charge of Dr Johnstone'. Arthur's few days in London in mid-May were 'utterly spoiled by absence from my darling wife combined with the fact that she was ill and I could not go to her'.

From 12-14 June Arthur was allowed to visit Louisa in Ilkley 'and at last after more than three months separation saw my darling again. She was looking very pale and thin'. He stayed with Dr Johnstone, and Louisa was able to walk out on the moor with him, morning and afternoon. He returned to Yorkshire again two weeks later, and was glad to find her looking much better. He brought her back to Cronkbourne with him on 30 June, Woodburn Place having been shut up during her illness. At last, on 7 July, they got back into their own house, four-and-a-half months after Helena's birth. A second, public, christening for the baby took place in November at Braddan Church.

In November Arthur was saddened to hear of the death of his old friend John Drinkwater Lawe (Appendix II, page 157). Christmas was spent at Cronkbourne in 1888, by which time Louisa had become pregnant again; this time preparations were made months ahead of the birth. On 20 June 1889 'we paid off our servants, except nurse, and shut up the house at Woodburn Place. L. and baby went to Andreas, I to Cronkbourne'. They enjoyed a week together in London in early July, with the Pearson family and others, including a day out at the Henley Regatta and an eight-mile row downriver to Marlow. They spent a second week with Louisa's brother, the Revd Joshua Hughes-Games the younger, and his wife, at Handsworth

Vicarage near Birmingham. The third week of their holiday was taken at Ilkley, walking on the moor and along the river. On 22 July Arthur left his wife and little Helena there and went back to Cronkbourne. Louisa had evidently taken to Ilkley, and stayed there until the birth of her second child, with Arthur visiting her for about a week in each month.

Another baby girl arrived on 27 September, about a fortnight early, and Arthur was informed by telegram 'both going on well'. He hared across to England on a boat sailing to Barrow the next day, then stayed in Ilkley and enjoyed sightseeing in Yorkshire during Louisa's month of convalescence. The baby was christened Margery Christian in Ilkley on 31 October, and the next day the Moores and their two daughters returned to the Island and to Woodburn Place.

The following year was less eventful, from a family point of view, apart from some minor illnesses. Closing the house at Woodburn Place in the summer seems to have become a ritual: on 2 August, again, 'L. and children went to Andreas, I to Cronkbourne'. A week later Arthur and Louisa set off for a fortnight in Scandinavia, travelling by ship from Hull to Kristiansand in southern Norway, then by rail to Christiania (now Oslo), Stockholm – with some sailing in the archipelago – and Copenhagen, back via Lübeck, Hamburg, Flushing, by boat to Queensborough in Kent, then to London and home by the usual route. This whirlwind tour must have been meticulously planned in advance. They were not the only globe-trotters in the family: William Fine Moore, now seventy-six, sailed from Liverpool to New York and Boston and back in the SS *City of Berlin* in the autumn, and much enjoyed his trip.

The House of Keys election took place in April 1891 (see Chapter 6), and Louisa left the Island to stay with friends in Dublin, presumably to avoid Arthur's electioneering. But a 'bilious cold' (16 April) had turned within two days into 'gastric catarrh'. Arthur hastened over to Dublin to find his wife under the care of a doctor and a nurse, 'decidedly better, though very weak. She had been dangerously ill for two days'. She remained weak, but was able to enjoy drives in the country with Arthur until their return home on 27 April. It may have been just as well that he had been re-elected to the Keys unopposed.

In mid-May 1891 the Moore family moved down, and across, the road to Woodbourne House, which would be their permanent family home for the rest of Arthur Moore's life.[6] 'Many things are still left to be completed, but it was no use waiting for our very dilatory landlord'. Arthur continued to travel, with and without Louisa: in August he enjoyed a ten-day tour of south-west Ireland with 260 Welshmen from the Cambrian Archaeological

Association and 110 Irishmen from the Royal Society of Antiquaries of Ireland, but broke it short to join Louisa in Dublin for a week of shopping and trips into the Wicklow hills.

In September, as an offshoot of one of his London trips, he spent a couple of days in Hampshire visiting Ingham Whitaker at Grayshott Hall near Liphook. Exploring the area, 'we then called on Lady Russell, the widow of the late Lord John Russell', who had been Prime Minister in the 1850s. It is likely that Moore was carrying a letter of introduction from the Governor of the Isle of Man, Spencer Walpole, who had written an official life of Lord John which was published in 1889. 'She is a charming old lady, and I had a most interesting talk with her'. He also met her daughter Lady Agatha Russell, 'a nice bright little woman', and 'a grandson, a callow youth at Trinity College, Cambridge' who is not named, and was probably only mentioned because he was at Trinity. However, the callow youth would become more famous than anyone else Moore met in his entire life, apart from King Edward VII. He was Bertrand Russell (1872-1970), philosopher and peace campaigner, one of the great men of the twentieth century.[7]

Arthur and Louisa both suffered from poor health in the winter of 1892, but their spirits were restored by a voyage to Lisbon in May, followed by a week in London. In September a week in the Lake District did Louisa much good; the dutiful Arthur took her for a twelve-mile row on Lake Windermere. In December Tom (T. E.) Brown, who had just come home from Clifton to live in the Island again, stayed with them for a few days – he was 'very jolly and pleasant', and became a good friend over the next few years.

Early in 1893 Arthur turned forty, and at about that time, or soon after, Louisa once more became pregnant. In May they visited Chester, then London again. Louisa shopped while Arthur was occupied with Church matters. They went to the theatre as usual (*Becket*, *Charley's Aunt* and *Diplomacy*), did the rounds of the art galleries, and visited the new Imperial Institute in South Kensington.

In September Woodbourne House was shut up, and Arthur escorted Louisa and the children to Ilkley before returning alone to Cronkbourne. He was delighted to receive a telegram on 7 October announcing the birth of a 'fine boy' weighing 91/2 lbs. The baby was christened William Arnold Christian just before Christmas. Arthur joined the rest of the family in Yorkshire during Louisa's month of convalescence, and brought them home with him on 10 November. The girls, now aged five and four, were a source of great pleasure; both took part in *The House That Jack Built*, a children's play acted at Cronkbourne at Christmas with Helena (now usually referred to as Helen) as 'the rat', and Margery as 'the maiden all forlorn'.

In January baby William caught a cold which developed into bronchitis and then convulsions. He died on 28 January. It was a terrible blow. Louisa was prostrate with grief, and Arthur felt unable to make any entry in his diary for several months; even then, his 'domestic' entries for 1894 were restricted to a few lines. The Moores were sustained by their Christian faith. Arthur felt that no one who had seen William die 'could have doubted in another and better life', and that his son was 'safe in the arms of Jesus'; this was a deeply felt, and not merely conventional, response to the family's bereavement. A further blow was the suicide of Louisa's brother Edgar, a surgeon aged twenty-four who had become addicted to morphia, in Sussex in April.[8] Arthur persuaded Louisa to go with her parents and sister Winifred for a month in Normandy in May and June, and she returned in somewhat better health and spirits. He tried his best to soldier on, but William's death would long overshadow family life. On the first anniversary of his death the Moores and their daughters took a cross to Braddan cemetery and placed it on the grave he shared with his aunt Florence.

The winter of 1895 was very severe. In February drifts of snow fourteen feet deep were reported on the Laxey road, and even Woodbourne House was snowed up for two days. Louisa's parents had now left the Island, with her father accepting an appointment as Vicar of Hull. In April Arthur took her to stay for a week in Leamington Spa, from where they visited Coventry, Kenilworth, Warwick, Stratford-on-Avon, Shrewsbury and Arthur's old school, Rugby. He had been introduced to a new sport, golf, in 1891, and in May he overdid it, straining himself so badly that he was in bed for two days in great pain; it was nearly ten days before he could walk again.

Meanwhile William Fine Moore's health had been getting worse. He took to his bed for three days at the end of May and then died, aged nearly eighty-one, after twenty years as an invalid. His funeral at Braddan New Church was a well-attended and moving occasion, at which 'the men from the works managed the bearing, which was exceedingly well done'. Under the terms of his will, Cronkbourne and its contents, gardens and grounds were left to his wife Hannah for her lifetime and were then to go to Arthur, who inherited all his father's other land and farms directly. He was now the sole owner of the family firm, from the profits of which he was instructed to pay his mother £2,000p.a. There were also legacies for the other surviving Moore children.[9]

Information about Arthur's siblings is scattered throughout his diary. In 1895 Edith, the eldest, was thirty-seven. She travelled to London quite often and was involved in charity work, but after her father's death she was, like so many Victorian spinsters, living with and looking after her mother.

Alice Dorothy, known as Dolly, who was thirty in 1895, had married Bassett Seckham, brother of her friend Violet Seckham, in London in 1888. They lived at Thorpelands, a country house near Northampton, and had several children. Bassett Seckham was an army officer, eventually Colonel. In 1901, on his father's death, he inherited Whittington Old Hall near Lichfield, and the family moved to live there.

Godfrey, Arthur's younger brother, now aged twenty-seven, had been educated at Harrow. In 1886-7 he trained as an engineer at the Crystal Palace School of Engineering in Sydenham, south London. Arthur visited him there in October 1886, finding him working in the South Tower; he was very impressed by the establishment and by its director. Godfrey started his working life at James Nasmyth's Bridgewater Foundry in Manchester, but in 1897 gained a permanent appointment as a civil engineer on the South India Railway. He married in India, started a family, and often turned up at Cronkbourne on home leave.

Margaret Rosamund, known in the family as Rosie, was twenty-four in 1895. Like her elder sister Edith, she lived with her mother at Cronkbourne, never married, and never followed a career. But the youngest sister, Katie Mildred (known as Mildred), was twenty-one when her father died, and probably a more spirited character. In 1891-2 she had been sent to Paris to be 'finished' at Madame Yeatman's Academy in Neuilly. She trained as a nurse, was working at Guy's Hospital from 1898 until at least 1900, and then from 1903 for the Bishop of Jerusalem. Later she would see distinguished service with the Red Cross in Serbia during the 1915 typhus epidemic, and in 1918 she was awarded the Royal Red Cross.

In 1895 Louisa became pregnant again, for the fourth time. In August she made her usual journey to Ilkley, and on 19 September Arthur gladly received a telegram saying 'Master Moore arrived this morning, all well'. He brought the two little girls and their nurse home from Yorkshire in mid-October. The baby was christened Arthur Hughes-Games Christian Moore in Ilkley, and they were all reunited in Douglas in mid-November. The family was now complete, and the three surviving children suffered no life-threatening emergencies. In the spring of 1896 Arthur (with or without Louisa is unknown) set off on another energetic foreign holiday – the first for four years – travelling to Spain by rail, taking in Bayonne, Biarritz, Pau and Lourdes in France before crossing the border to visit San Sebastian, Burgos and Madrid, then heading south to Seville, Cordoba and Granada.

In July a supper was held in Cronkbourne schoolhouse to celebrate the coming-of-age of the Cronkbourne Cricket Club (although in fact it was the twentieth rather than the twenty-first anniversary) and Arthur Moore, as the founder, was presented with a bat bearing a silver plate. Alas, the bat was broken a year later in a match against King William's College. In August first Louisa and then, with initial reluctance, Arthur, acquired bicycles. He wrote, 'I am now only sorry that I did not take it up long ago, as I find it most convenient for going to Cronkbourne and back'. Before long he was using his bicycle for much longer journeys. Louisa probably did not, and it seems unlikely that they took their cycles with them when visiting North Wales for a week in September, taking a return journey on the SS *Manxman* to Llandudno. Their ascent of Snowdon on 21 September was no doubt assisted by the newly-opened Mountain Railway.

The first six months of 1897 were very busy, including the Manx General Election and the celebration of Queen Victoria's Golden Jubilee (see Chapter 8). But there was time for a tour of the Loire valley in April and a visit to Canterbury in June, after staying the night with another clerical brother of Louisa's, the Revd Stephen Hughes-Games, vicar of Doddington in Kent.

In July Arthur became a more serious cyclist and experienced some of the hazards involved. He set out on the 8th with young Mr Heap, a new friend from Liverpool with whose father he had stayed while attending the British Association the previous year. They headed towards Bishopscourt via Injebreck, but when they got to the shepherd's hut near Druidale 'it came on a tremendous downpour of rain, so we turned back and came home ten miles via Pen-y-Pot in 55 minutes, arriving home drenched to the skin'. A worse mishap occurred on the 26th: 'Went on my bicycle to Park Llewellyn to see how the new fence is progressing. On my return, owing to the steering gear jamming in a mysterious way, I ran into the stone wall at Creg-ny-baa turn instead of turning the corner (my feet were up at the time) and was thrown off the bicycle, stunned and pretty badly cut about. However I managed to pull the bicycle and myself together and got home somehow. I felt the effects for three weeks afterwards and it will be a lesson to me not to 'coast' around a corner again!'

On 14 August, at the invitation of the directors of the Tramway Company, Moore enjoyed a more sedentary event, the ascent of Snaefell by the newly-built mountain railway. The party included the Hall Caines and the Manx-American poet Henry Hanby Hay, whom he found excessively deferential and flattering. The weather was appalling, but the dinner in the summit hotel was 'very pleasant and lively', and they got back about 10pm. On 19 August he had recovered sufficiently from his accident to cycle to lunch at Bishopscourt and back, via Ramsey and Park Llewellyn, a forty-mile run with a head wind on the way home via Pen-y-Pot.

The year ended more sombrely, with the deaths of T. E. Brown in Bristol in late October and Uncle John Pearson in London in early December. Arthur and his mother travelled to London for Pearson's funeral, held in Westminster Abbey where he was buried. Now seldom remembered, John Pearson was an eminent figure in his lifetime. Arthur and Hannah Moore stayed with Uncle Henry Christian at 18 Devonshire Place, Marylebone, not far from the Pearson home.

In 1898 Hannah was ill with 'rheumatism of the sciatic nerve', and spent some months in Harrogate for the good of her health; Louisa and the children spent time there with her. Arthur left them, took his bicycle with him on the train to Newmarket and enjoyed a week in Suffolk and Norfolk, his first proper cycling holiday. He managed a week in Oxford and London in October, but all the other events of the year would pale into insignificance compared with his election as Speaker of the House of Keys in December.

In 1899 Moore's life would become even busier, due to his increased public responsibilities and the many calls upon his time. There were also additional responsibilities relating to the firm; in February he began 'the necessary and long delayed work of pulling down some of the older houses in Cronkbourne Village and building new ones'. An Easter touring holiday with Louisa included visits to Bath, Bradford-on-Avon, Wells Cathedral, Bournemouth and Christchurch. One afternoon Arthur walked alone to Boscombe, where his mother was staying, attended as always by Edith and Rosie. Hannah Moore was looking well, but was semi-paralysed, as she continued to be for the rest of her life. 'She cannot get out of her chair, or walk across a room without help'. She was now seventy-two. Arthur and Louisa returned home via London.

'From 31st May-22nd June I had a delightful bicycling tour in Brittany and the Channel Islands'. The tour included Guernsey and Jersey, then went on to Granville on the French coast, where Moore had to obtain a cycling permit before proceeding to Avranches and Mont St Michel ('good beyond expectation') and then, by a mixture of train, boat and bicycle, making his way round almost the entire coastline of the Breton peninsula, including the major prehistoric monuments.

In early July, en route to the National Eisteddfod at Cardiff, he visited Worcester, Hereford and Malvern. An exceptionally warm August ended with a large party at Government House, invited to meet the singer Miss Clara Butt. 'I sat next to her and found her amusing, but rather vulgar. She is an enormous woman, being over six feet high'. In early September Arthur and Louisa took young Arthur, now five, for a week in the Lakes. The razzamatazz and fuss about fund-raising for the Boer War around the Island in

December appears to have left Moore cool and sceptical.

The year 1900 began with further grumbles about 'this wretched war' and the news that Bassett Seckham, Dolly's husband and a major in the Staffordshire Militia, had been summoned to go to South Africa (there is no more about this in Moore's diary, but if Seckham did go to the war, he survived). The collapse of Dumbell's Bank was the major, and disastrous, event in the Island that year, and it involved Arthur Moore in further anxiety since in 1899 he had joined the board of the Isle of Man Bank, now affected by rumours about its own stability. He also accepted office as a director of the Steam Packet Company in February, which involved fairly frequent trips to meetings in Liverpool, or to witness the trials of new boats.

Hannah Moore was spending some of her time in a flat in London, just off Baker Street, still attended by her two faithful spinster daughters. 'She is almost an absolute cripple. Edith looks very tired and worn, Rosie much as usual'. At the end of June Moore attended the funeral of Lord Loch in Suffolk with Sir James Gell, as the Island's official representatives. Of Loch he recalled, 'He made me a magistrate when I was only 23 and was always a kind and good friend'. This was a burdensome year, in which Moore's *History of the Isle of Man* was at last finished and published.

But Arthur still found some time for bicycling and golf, for five days staying at Tunbridge Wells and cycling in Sussex in April, combined with the usual few days in London. He and Louisa enjoyed a fortnight in and around Killarney in September, but when he got home he was too busy to keep up his diary for the last three months of the year.

With all this pressure of public events, the space devoted to private and family matters in Moore's diary diminishes. His growing involvement with the Pan-Celtic movement (Chapter 7) was another pressure on his time. The queen's death in January 1901 was followed towards the end of the month by Louisa suffering an attack of diphtheria; Margery and young Arthur were sent up to Willaston to be looked after by the Rings, so as to be kept free from the danger of infection. Fortunately Louisa soon recovered, thanks to the ministrations of Dr Hamilton, but the children did not come home until 18 February.

Arthur and Louisa spent ten days in Belgium in May and June, and in early July Arthur managed a few days in the New Forest, while he was in Southampton inspecting a boat which was a possible purchase for the Steam Packet Company. The Glasgow International Exhibition, with its semi-oriental buildings, machinery and 'the best and most comprehensive exhibition of modern art I have ever seen brought together' (including English, French and Belgian painters), merited a rushed thirty-hour visit.

This, undertaken with Louisa, included two rough passages by boat between Douglas and Ardrossan, and an evening theatre visit in Glasgow. No one could accuse the Moores, cushioned though they might be from hardship, of lacking energy or vigour, but it is notable how little holiday time they enjoyed in 1901 compared with previous years.

The year 1902 started with some pleasant events. On 2 January the Moores took the Governor's box at the Gaiety Theatre to see *The Mikado* performed by the Douglas Choral Society. 'It was very well done. The first time for Helen and Margery to go to the theatre. They enjoyed themselves immensely'. In February they also went to see *King Gob-ne-Geay*, a Manx comic opera by William Hanby, with music by Harry Wood, using the ballads and songs assembled in the books by Moore and W. H. Gill. Arthur thought the scenery was good, some of the acting (mainly by children) very creditable, and the acrobatics excellent.[10]

At the end of January, in Liverpool on Steam Packet business, he addressed some 2,000 members of the Liverpool Manx Society in St George's Hall. He only spoke for twenty minutes, and thought he was fairly well heard, but found it a great strain speaking in such a large hall.

In May Arthur and Louisa went to stay with her parents in Hull, then to London in bitterly cold weather, and finally to Cheltenham on 22 May. This was not sightseeing; Helen was to start as a pupil at Cheltenham Ladies' College after midsummer. They were shown around the school by the celebrated headmistress, Miss Dorothea Beale, 'a truly wonderful energetic old lady', then toured some half-dozen boarding houses in the town, finally selecting one for Helen kept by the Misses Croft, 'connections of Archbishop Benson's, and my old tutor, Arthur Sidgwick'.

The summer of 1902 was unusually fraught with public events involving Arthur Moore. He and Louisa went to London in June for the coronation of King Edward VII, which had to be postponed due to the king's illness, and then had to rush home for the funeral of the Island's Governor, Lord Henniker. A return boat trip to Kirkcudbright at the end of July gave Arthur the chance of a day's cycling via Dundrennan and Castle Douglas while the rest of the party went by coach. The excitements of the coronation in London followed on 9 August, and the unexpected visit by the king and his entourage to the Isle of Man on 24-25 August. In September Lord Raglan arrived unofficially – Arthur and Louisa drove him over to Bishopscourt, where he stayed – and in October he was formally installed as Governor.

Arthur was back in south-west Scotland for a further day's cycling round Wigtown Bay and Gatehouse of Fleet at the end of August, perhaps to unwind after the royal visit. Meanwhile in September all the Moores' three children started at new schools: Margery at Milntown near Ramsey, which was run by the Revd William Bell Christian's widow Sophia (known as 'Vio'), Arthur at Miss Cowen's, and Helen at Cheltenham, to which she was escorted by her father. Since he was there, he hired a bicycle for a few days in Oxfordshire and Worcestershire. In November Arthur Moore had his portrait painted in London by Charles Goldsborough Anderson, a society artist with a studio in the Fulham Road who regularly exhibited at the Royal Academy. In the same month Aunt Sarah Christian died of heart failure – her body was brought back to the Isle of Man by Frank Pearson, his wife Cecilia ('Cissie') and Uncle Henry Christian, to be buried in Braddan Cemetery. A tumultuous year ended with Christmas at Cronkbourne and *The Gondoliers* at the Gaiety.

Arthur Moore's diaries invariably emphasise holidays and other highlights because that was what he enjoyed writing about, and because he did not write in his diary every day – only when he had time and thought he had something worthwhile to record. He was a very busy man, heavily burdened with responsibilities despite his enviable holidays, and the strain was beginning to show. But there was life in him yet; he recorded with satisfaction on 1 January 1903 that he had ridden 2,100 miles on his bicycle in the preceding two years. On 6 February: 'My 50th birthday. I never thought I would attain a half-century!' For the remainder of his life, his stamina would be tested as never before.

Two views of Woodbourne House (now part of the Masonic Hall in Douglas), which Arthur and Louisa Moore rented from the Todhunter family for most of their married life. Expecting one day to inherit Cronkbourne, Arthur would have had no reason to buy another property.

The hall and anteroom at Cronkbourne in 1890. The brief visit by King Edward VII and Queen Alexandra in 1902 was subsequently commemorated by an inscription carved on the hall fireplace.

These views of the main reception rooms at Cronkbourne were taken in 1890, when Arthur Moore's parents were both still alive. The style of furnishing, complete with Turkey rugs, 'parlour palms', bamboo tables, screens and elaborate drapery, would reflect the taste of Hannah Moore rather than that of her son and daughter-in-law, who never lived here as man and wife.

The east facade of Cronkbourne in 1902; this view from the opposite bank of the the River Glass shows an ornamental pool and fountain which is still in the garden. The photograph of 'Murphy, head gardener, in the fernery' is undated, but Arthur Moore mentions James Murphy twice in his diary for 1884; he won prizes at the Floral, Horticultural and Rose Society's annual show in that, and no doubt other, years. The picture of the elegant landau is captioned in the family album 'Welsh, last of the Cronkbourne coachmen'.

Chapter 5

AUTHOR

The process of historical research and writing is obsessive, absorbing, sometimes exhausting. Those who are doing it do not usually add to their labours by keeping a journal in which to write about what they are writing. Thus tracing the development of Arthur Moore's scholarly interests and activities is not entirely straightforward.

Quine tells us that in 1879 Moore began going through parish registers, which in those days were kept in the rectories and vicarages of the Island, in search of Manx surnames. This may have been linked to his research into the Moore genealogy and on 'Old Manx Families' more generally, which resulted in an unpublished text of that name, completed in 1881.[1] He may initially have been enthused enough to get involved in serious research by family pride and even a degree of ancestor-worship – not that these motives always guarantee scrupulous objectivity.[2] But his research on names took him beyond his own family history into correspondence with others in the field. In June 1882, for instance, he called on Canon Isaac Taylor, author of *Words and Places*, with whom he had previously corresponded on Manx place names, at Settrington Rectory in North Yorkshire. Taylor was later a contributor to the *Manx Note Book*.

It was also in 1882 that Moore joined the Isle of Man Natural History and Antiquarian Society (IoMNHAS), which had been founded in December 1879 with P. M. C. Kermode as the moving spirit, and which by 1883 boasted some fifty members, rising during Moore's lifetime to about 200.[3] The existence of such a gentlemanly antiquarian society in the Isle of Man provided an environment, an audience and an outlet for publications through which Moore could share his scholarly enthusiasms with others.[4]

The list of twenty-nine papers and reports which he delivered to the IoMNHAS between 1883 and 1908 gives some idea of the range and catholicity of his interests.[5] He also contributed annual weather reports, short pieces on exceptional weather events, and the occasional book review to the Society's journal *Yn Lioar Manninagh* – for example a review of Kermode's *Manx Crosses* in 1892. In the Society's early years it was the usual custom to combine a summer field trip to sites of botanical, archaeological or historical interest with a picnic, if the weather was good, and the reading of one or two short papers in the open air, perhaps at some convenient vicarage or country house such as Cronkbourne. As Moore was a busy public man, particularly after he entered the Keys in 1885, and even more so after he became Speaker in 1898, on nine occasions papers authored by him were read by others in his absence. But he played an active part in the Society, leading excursions to Marown in 1892 and to Baldwin in 1900, as a committee member from 1886 to 1895, and as President for the year 1892-3. The importance of the IoMNHAS in providing an opportunity for Moore to air his ideas and findings, explore new subjects and publish papers, should not be underestimated.

His first distinctive contribution to the Island's culture, which brought him to the attention of a wider public than the members of the IoMNHAS, was the quarterly journal which he announced at the end of July 1884, and which he edited throughout its life of twelve issues in three years (1885-7). The three volumes of the *Manx Note Book*, which were illustrated by John Miller Nicholson and beautifully produced, are still a pleasure both to read and to handle.

This was a short-lived but influential publication. Launched with a preface by the Governor, Spencer Walpole, himself a scholar and historian, the journal announced its aim as 'to preserve and maintain the monuments, traditions, names, folklore and history of the Isle of Man'. Walpole's preface referred to the 'promoters' and 'projectors' of the magazine, but only Moore's name appeared as editor. It is possible that Walpole himself was among the journal's backers. The *Manx Note Book* was an avowedly antiquarian publication, including short factual articles on a wide variety of Manx subjects. It was also intended to be a forum for controversy and debate, to stimulate further research and publication, and to challenge the existing inactive state of Manx scholarship. The July 1885 number carried a letter from the young William Cubbon, then aged just twenty, pointedly asking 'What is the Manx Society for the Publication of National Documents doing lately?'

Like so many promising Manx journals, the *Note Book*, which cost ten shillings a year, could not generate a readership large enough to break even, and closed after three years. But during its brief existence it provided a forum in which Moore and others could publish short articles, many of which would be followed up and expanded into the books which he wrote during the following fifteen years or so. The *Note Book* included a series of papers on Manx surnames, notes on Manx superstitions, Manx ballads, articles on old Manx families, a debate about the runes on Manx crosses, and a series, by Moore and others, on 'Manx Worthies'.

The publication was generally very well received, but it and its editor were not to everyone's taste. This is what T. E. Brown had to say in a letter written in October 1885: 'Poor Arthur Moore may work away at his old soakless, screeching, rusty-fusty archaeological pump for ever, and he'll get up a lot of sound like enough: but it is nothing to what you can get, simply by going to the living heart of the actual living people. If a man's contemporaries are not to him the matter of supreme interest, then he better attend to "double entry" and the rest of it'.[6] Brown later took a different and much more positive view of Moore.

In fact Arthur Moore's research did involve him with living people. For example, on 7 March 1885 'went with W. J. Cain to see John Quirk of Carn-y-Greie, Patrick (Glen Rushen). He had not been more than a few miles from home for many years. His last visit to Douglas was in 1825, and to Peel in 1830. He is now 85 years old and very feeble. He has a very fine face and notwithstanding his seclusion, takes great interest in the affairs of the outer world. Though uneducated he has composed several poems, and has made some good translations from Manx ballads'. In his entry on Quirk in *Manx Worthies*, Moore recounts how 'when [I] told [John Quirk] of [my] love for all things Manx and of [my] desire to hear him read some of his carols, his face at once lit up, as he took down his MSS from the "latt" and complied with the request'. Quirk died later that year.[7] Cain was, like Moore, a Manx language enthusiast. He was also the Braddan parish clerk, and one of Moore's collaborators on the book of *Manx Carols* or *Carvallyn Gailckagh*, to be published in 1891. Here we catch a rare glimpse of the two men involved in the processes of cultural fieldwork, retrieval and recording.

Admittedly, most of the people met in the course of Moore's research, whom he recorded in his diary, were fellow antiquarians. Thus, at the end of October 1885: '22nd. Left at 12 and drove over to Ballaugh Rectory where I lunched. Rev. W. Kermode and E. B. Savage, Dr Tellet, and P. M. C. Kermode there. We discuss the subject of Manx Place names'. '24th To Castletown. Call on old Mr Kewley at the Rolls office and arrange about examining old documents there. 29th Examined documents as arranged'.

But a great deal of his scholarly work was done with visiting scholars based outside the Island. It was as though the *Manx Note Book* acted as a catalyst in drawing the Isle of Man to the attention of a number of eminent authorities in different fields. They included the anthropologist and ethnographer John Beddoe (1826-1911), the geologist and antiquarian Professor William Boyd Dawkins (1837-1929) of Owens College, later Manchester

University, John Rhys (1840-1915), Professor of Celtic Studies at Oxford, and Gudbrandr Vigfusson (1827-1889), Reader in Icelandic Language and Literature at Oxford, who took a special interest in the Island's runic crosses. All these men visited the Isle of Man, in most cases for the first time, in the summer of 1886.[8]

Moore recorded in his diary: 'July 27 – met Profs. Boyd Dawkins and Rhys and Dr Beddoe at dinner at Mr Savage's. I found them all very interesting men'. The Revd Ernest B. Savage, vicar of St Thomas's Church, Douglas, was an especially keen antiquarian. On the following two days they all went out together on excursions to the Baldwin valleys and to Sulby, where Beddoe and Savage went on a 'head measuring tour' and claimed to find 'rather more of the Scandinavian type at the North than at the South of the Island'.

On 31 July Moore was appointed to the newly-created committee of Ancient Monuments Trustees, who began their work on 12 August when 'Mr Kneale and I were deputed to make out a list of Antiquities'. This was done in response to an official report on Manx antiquities written by Boyd Dawkins for Governor Walpole in 1885, and reprinted in the *Manx Note Book* in January 1886. Moore was also stimulated to press on with his own research: on 18 August he lunched at Bridge House, Castletown, 'and afterwards went through a number of documents copied from the records by the various Quayles who were Clerks of the Rolls'.

Boyd Dawkins was still, or again, on the Island in late August when 'we walked over to Braddan and inspected the crosses and the alignment in the plantation on Kirby farm'. The next day, with Savage, they 'geologised' from Derbyhaven to Cass-ny-Howin, carefully noting the distribution of slate and conglomerate. A month later Dr Vigfusson, another 'very interesting man', arrived in the Island. 'He speaks English very indifferently'. He lunched or dined with the Moores on three occasions in late September and early October, was very pleased to find an additional inscription on one of the crosses at Kirk Michael, and inspected the crosses at Braddan with Moore; they then went to call on the Governor.

Professor Rhys was back again in the summer of 1887 when he, with Moore and Savage, enjoyed a pleasant excursion on 2 July to Lonan Old Church and Kirk Michael in search of Ogham markings on stones and crosses. They inspected the northern Tynwald site at Reneurling, and afterwards went to Clyeen farmhouse where 'its owner Killip – a very intelligent and pleasant man – entertained us to a sumptuous banquet consisting of tea, milk, rhubarb jam and scones. He read a chapter in the Manx Bible to us'. Vigfusson, too, was back in October 'to revise his readings of the runes'.

Meanwhile a party from the British Association for the Advancement of Science arrived on their first visit to the Island in September. 'About 80 came. A more uninviting set of persons I have seldom seen'. Boyd Dawkins led them in an excursion from their conference in Manchester.

Boyd Dawkins' 1885 report on the Island's antiquities had stressed the importance of studying and preserving remains which could illuminate 'the complicated and little-known relation of the Northmen to the Celtic population of the British Isles'. This was a major point of interest and dispute for scholars concerned with the Isle of Man, in the 1880s and later. It was the key issue for John Beddoe in his study of 'The Physical Anthropology of the Isle of Man', an early version of which appeared in the *Manx Note Book* in January 1887; Moore collaborated with Beddoe on successive later versions. Vigfusson entered into the debate about Manx crosses, claiming them for the Scandinavian tradition (*Manx Note Book*, January 1887), but his contribution to Manx scholarship was curtailed by his death in 1889. It was John Rhys whose interest in the Island was sustained the longest, and who became Moore's lifelong friend and collaborator. Rhys had been invited to the Isle of Man in 1886 by Savage 'to inspect the ancient ogham inscriptions'. He was introduced by Savage to Moore, and also to W. J. Cain, who read Manx to him for the first time. Rhys began to take a serious interest in learning the Manx language, and visited the Island a further five times from 1888 to 1893 in pursuit of his studies, often staying with the Moores.[9]

The mid-1880s were crucial years in bringing the Island and its antiquities to the notice of a wider world of British scholars and antiquarians. This was not the work of Moore alone, but he, with his wide range of interests, first class history degree and resources of time and money, was the man on the spot best qualified to follow through with a series of solid research-based monographs.

During the next few years, after the demise of the *Manx Note Book*, his diary is chiefly concerned with domestic matters, particularly the births of his daughters. One enjoyable trip, however, a visit to Oxford in October 1888 to stay with John Rhys and his family, was related to his scholarly pursuits. Rhys showed him round several Oxford colleges and introduced him to the pioneering economic historian Dr J. E. Thorold Rogers, who had visited Milntown and stayed with Deemster John Christian forty years earlier, and the anthropologist Dr Edward Burnett Tylor. Later he dined in the Jesus College Common Room, and met several other dons including Dr James Murray the lexicographer and William R. Morfill, scholar in Slavonic languages. It was 'a most delightful evening', and possibly reminded him of the kind of alternative career he could have had.

The next morning he went to Dr Murray's 'Scriptorium', where he and his assistants were at work compiling the *Oxford English Dictionary*. 'They had just reached the work "checkmate" and Dr M. showed me all the quotations about it which he had received. He had 41/2 million references to all the different words written on slips which were placed in the pigeonholes which nearly covered the walls of the room'. Rhys and Moore then went to the Clarendon Press where they had a long discussion with the Director about their proposed new edition of Bishop Phillips' Manx Prayer Book, a project which was to come to fruition in 1893-4. Moore also looked at the various processes of printing books in half a dozen different languages. The whole visit was a highly enjoyable taste of academic life at Oxford.

During 1888 and 1889 he was presumably working on his *Manx Names, or the Surnames and Place-Names of the Isle of Man*, published by Elliott Stock, London, with a list of subscribers. It appeared in July 1890 with an introduction by John Rhys, who wrote that he had urged Moore to place on record the fruits of his familiarity with the official records of the Island. This short book was based mainly on the scrutiny of parish registers, which Moore had started in 1879, for surnames, and he expressed his thanks to the rectors and vicars of the Island; for help with place names he acknowledged the work of the place-names committee of the IoMNHAS. Thanks were expressed to Rhys, Vigfusson, and to other scholars including Henry Bradley, one of the editors of the *Oxford English Dictionary*. Moore's book is clearly written and efficiently organised. His analysis of the data he had collected led him to the conclusion that within the overall Scandio-Celtic character of the population, 'Between sixty and seventy per cent of the Manx place-names are of Goidelic [i.e. Irish Gaelic] origin, almost twenty per cent being Scandinavian, and the rest English'. The book earned 'a very favourable review in the *Saturday* [*Review*]'. An anonymous five-page review in *Yn Lioar Manninagh* made a number of detailed criticisms, and these led to corrections in the second edition, published in 1902, which acknowledged help from scholars including P. M. C. Kermode, John Quine and Charles Roeder. There was a third, cheap, revised edition in 1906. Moore was always very willing to accept and to learn from the scholarship of others. He was an academic trailblazer, here and in most of his books. His work was the first word on its subject, not the last. From 1897 on he encouraged the work of the young man who was to continue his efforts in this field, J. J. Kneen, who dedicated his *The Place-Names of the Isle of Man* (1925) to Moore, and later went on to produce *The Personal Names of the Isle of Man* (1937).[10]

Moore's second book, *The Folk-Lore of the Isle of Man*, was published hard on the heels of the first, in the summer of 1891. By modern standards this book is unattractively presented, with a cramped typeface. But it is a rich collection of myths, superstitions, fairies, hobgoblins, monsters, giants, customs like hunting the wren, old proverbs and sayings, which still makes good reading more than a century after its publication. Extended quotations from earlier writers in Moore's introduction provide a compelling sketch of Manx rural society since the sixteenth century. He argues that the study of folklore is 'often the only possible means of penetrating to the historic past of nations' and is, in effect, the way to an understanding of Manx social history. The help of John Rhys and Alfred Nutt (1856-1901), a founder of the Folklore Society, is acknowledged, along with the 'many kind friends who have contributed scraps of Folk-Lore', much of it from oral sources. Moore can sometimes seem far removed from the life of the Manx common people of his day, but not in this book. He continued to publish further work on folklore, including 'Further Notes on Manx Folklore', a series of articles in *The Antiquary* for 1895, which were then republished by S. K. Broadbent as a booklet, *Manx Folklore*, in 1899. In the first volume of his *Bibliography of the Isle of Man*, published in 1933, William Cubbon has no hesitation in describing Moore's 1891 account as 'the standard work on Manx folklore'. Despite the publication of a more modern work, also called *The Folklore of the Isle of Man*, by Margaret Killip in 1975, Moore's book is still essential; it was republished in facsimile in 1994.

One consequence of Moore's growing reputation as a writer on Manx subjects was his increasing attendance at congresses and conferences on the subjects which interested him, and invitations to give papers. Thus in October 1891 he is to be found at the International Folk-Lore Congress in London, held in the rooms of the Society of Antiquaries at Burlington House, Piccadilly. He was there for the Congress opening on 1 October, and was introduced to the President, Andrew Lang, 'a good-looking man, evidently with a very active brain', and several other luminaries. A collection of objects was on display, and Moore showed photographs of the Ballafletcher Luck Cup, the Sicilian Three Legs, and Tynwald Hill. He did not attend all six days of the Congress, and found some papers very dull, but was encouraged by John Rhys's lecture on mythology and enjoyed an evening entertainment at the Mercers' Hall, 'when representations were given of mumming, playing children's games etc.' On the last day he read his paper on the Tynwald Hill, attended the official dinner, and left by the midnight train.

The year 1891 was marked by the publication of *Carvallyn Gailckagh*, a collection of Manx carols with English translations which Moore edited. It included eighty-five carvals, several of them dating from the early eighteenth century, and many put into print for the first time. John Quirk, whom Moore had interviewed in 1885 and who was the source of several of them, 'was probably the last remaining specimen of the kind of men who composed the Manx carols'. In producing this book, Moore collaborated with W. J. Cain, the publisher J. C. Fargher, also editor of the *Mona's Herald*, and R. E. Christian, a retired sea captain living in Maughold, who was responsible for the translations.[11] Moore also corresponded with, among many others, G. W. Wood, the noted Manx bibliophile who lived in London, throughout the 1890s.[12]

Various kinds of history-related activities occupied him during 1892. At the end of January the Ancient Monuments Trustees, who from their foundation in 1886 had also been entrusted with the task of setting up a national museum, decided to establish it at Castle Rushen, with the proviso that nothing specially given for a Douglas museum should be sent there. In May Moore was elected as President of the IoMNHAS. In June he was pleased when the Manx Society, which had been virtually moribund, decided to publish Bishop Phillips' Prayer Book, with himself and John Rhys as editors. In December he published an article in the *Isle of Man Times* on 'The Early Land System of the Isle of Man', one of his many papers to the IoMNHAS, and numerous newspaper articles.

The next substantial publication of Moore's was his book on *The Diocese of Sodor and Man*, which appeared in 1893 as one of a series of diocesan histories published by the Society for the Promotion of Christian Knowledge. Cubbon, in 1933, described it as the standard history of the Manx Church, and yet again the claim still seems to be tenable today. Canon John Gelling's *A History of the Manx Church 1698-1911*, published in 1998, is an invaluable source of references and of detailed information on individual parishes, clergy and bishops, but it covers a shorter timespan than Moore's book, and was not originally intended for publication. Moore's is a succinct account of the whole period from the fifth to the nineteenth centuries. He acknowledged help from the Clerk of the Rolls, the Vicar-General, his father-in-law the Archdeacon, and also from Bishop Stubbs of Oxford – eminent both as a churchman and a historian – and John Frowde. Frowde was an enthusiastic antiquarian and collector of Manxiana who worked as the librarian of Bermondsey and consulted manuscripts in the British Museum on Moore's behalf. This history has attracted less attention than some of Moore's other works, but it was an important expression of his devoted Anglicanism. More surprisingly this book, written in an ecumenical and fair-minded spirit, also includes a chapter on the rise of Methodism. Moore found it easier to understand and take seriously the Wesleyans, as opposed to the Primitive Methodists, but he took a general interest in the nonconformist denominations and from this time on did not shun invitations to speak at Methodist and Presbyterian events.

Just as Moore's book on folklore was followed by attendance at the Folk-Lore Congress, so the publication of his book on the Manx Church, which was warmly received in the diocese, may have had something to do with a period of greater public involvement in the Church of England on his part. Arthur Moore was very occupied with Church matters during the spring and early summer, as a member of the House of Laymen in the Church of England Synod at Easter in York, though a visit to Durham Cathedral made more impression on him than the meetings, in which he was 'not particularly interested' as he knew no one there except Lord Cross, the chairman, whose son had been at Rugby with him. 'The whole affair had such an air of unreality', he later told John Quine. He went to a service for the House of Laymen in London in May, to a rally in the Albert Hall against the disestablishment of the Welsh Church, and to a reception given at Lambeth Palace by the Archbishop of Canterbury, E. W. Benson. But in the opinion of some Anglicans he was not reliably orthodox: in October 1894 he caused a sensation at the Diocesan Conference by the liberal views he expressed in a paper on Sunday observance (see Chapter 6).

In 1895 the two-volume edition of *The Book of Common Prayer in Manx Gaelic*, edited by Moore and Rhys, at last appeared, jointly published by the Manx Society, whose last publication it was, and Oxford University Press. Vol. I included, in addition to the texts of translations made by Bishop Phillips in 1610, and by the Manx clergy in 1765, a preface by Rhys, and a biographical memoir of Bishop Phillips and description of the manuscripts, both by Moore. Vol. II was devoted to Manx translations of the Psalms, appendices, and a disquisition on 'The Outlines of the Phonology of Manx Gaelic' by John Rhys. The work was a scholarly labour of love, clearly destined for a small, highly-educated, specialist readership.

In 1896 Arthur Moore was selected by the IoMNHAS as their delegate to the British Association for the Advancement of Science conference to be held in Liverpool in September. He stayed for nearly a week with Mr R. Heap of West Derby, a wealthy rice merchant who lived in a fine house in large grounds which contained a number of vineries and orchid houses.[13] He attended the opening address by the President of the BAAS, Sir Joseph Lister, on anaesthetics, which he found very interesting but almost entirely inaudible. He thought much the same of an address by the archaeologist Sir Arthur Evans. He went to hear various papers on anthropology, geology and geography, and to a soirée given by the Lord Mayor, Lord Derby, in the Town Hall. The place was 'crowded to suffocation' with, Moore estimated, more than 3,000 people, and he was pleased to meet Fred Caröe, the younger brother of W. D. Caröe, and his wife.

As in 1887, Moore was again rather snobbish about the members of the British Association. On Friday 18th he read his paper 'The Physical Anthropology of the Isle of Man', which was well received, and in the afternoon went – with some 1,000 others – to a garden party at Lord Derby's seat at Knowsley. He and Deemster Gill, 'wisely refraining from mingling with the Mob which was waiting to be introduced', walked round the grounds for some time before approaching Lord and Lady Derby. Lord Derby invited Moore to come back on the Monday and look through Stanley family papers connected with the Isle of Man, which he did with Philip (P. M. C.) Kermode, who also had permission. Lord Derby and his librarian showed them 'the Manx Papers' which consisted, according to Moore, mostly of uninteresting law cases, with some more important papers concerning the Island's revenue in the seventeenth and eighteenth centuries. He went back again a year later, in September 1897, when he spent two days working on the documents at Knowsley, and was satisfied that he had missed nothing of any importance.

As before, a party of about 100 British Association people visited the Isle of Man after their conference, at the end of September 1896. Arthur Moore invited a few of the leading lights to dinner: Professor Alfred C. Haddon (1855–1940), the zoologist and anthropologist, with his wife, and Alice Gomme (1853-1938), who had been a founding member of the Folk-Lore Society. He and Louisa went to meet the delegation at a garden party at Government House, and once more he observed: 'They had come straight up from the steamer and certainly looked a queer and dishevelled set!' The Moores also joined the party at a dinner at the Sefton Hotel: 'The dinner was a poor one and the speeches after it, for the most part, were indifferent'.

Towards the end of the year, on 20 November, 'My Book of Manx Ballads [was] at last published', about which he felt more enthusiastic. *Manx Ballads and Music*, again illustrated by John Miller Nicholson, was printed in an edition of 500 copies by G. and R. Johnson of Douglas. It includes seventy-four Manx ballads, with English translations, nearly half of them accompanied by the old tunes which had been harmonised by Miss M. L. Wood 'the mother of Manx music'.[14] There is a preface by T. E. Brown and a scholarly introduction of more than twenty pages by Moore, who may have got more sheer enjoyment from the preparation of this book than from any of his others. This was because ever since 1892 he had been corresponding about it with T. E. Brown. The two men became firm friends; Brown was a welcome visitor to the Moore household, and soon revised the unfavourable view of Moore he had held in 1885. A letter of Brown's in December 1892 says, 'Moore is deeply interested in Manx history and antiquities. So we got on splendidly together'. Incidentally, he reveals quite how assiduous a researcher Moore was: 'At Copenhagen, in the museum, he examined the papers of an old Danish professor who died somewhere about 1750 ... and found a Manx song, with English translation, by Archdeacon Rutter ... in about 1680'.[15] This must have been during Moore's fortnight on tour in Scandinavia with Louisa in August 1890. One wonders what she thought about it.

By November 1894 Brown was praising Moore to the skies: 'I fancy your book will be a very taking one. What a lot of good work you will have done for the Island, and that while still young! When you come to my age... You will then be the great authority on things Manx. That is a responsibility which you will regard as supremely incumbent on you, a responsibility and an honour... Persevere to the end'. He would.[16]

Manx Ballads and Music is a book which places a high value on scholarly accuracy. It was not entirely comprehensive; Moore omitted erotic ballads which were 'too gross and indecent for publication' and also ballads written in the previous fifty years, largely temperance songs which he considered to consist of 'the most inferior type of doggerel'.[17] W. H. Gill's *Manx National Song Book*, also published in 1896, was a very different kind of publication, intended to popularise Manx songs in English versions, some of them newly invented, and avoiding the use of the Manx language. Moore's book, virtually unavailable for many years, was reprinted in facsimile in 1998.

During the next four years references in his diary to Moore's cultural and historical interests are few and far between. In June 1897 his paper on 'The Physical Anthropology of the Isle of Man', previously delivered to the British Association, was read again, this time to the Anthropological Society in London, by someone else deputising for Moore in his absence. The paper, credited jointly to Moore and Beddoe, was published in August in the *Journal of the Anthropological Institute*. It was an attempt to tabulate the physical characteristics of 1,112 Manxmen over the age of eighteen who had served in the Royal Fencibles between 1803 and 1810, and to categorize them by parish and ethnic origin. In October he was interested enough to take a look at the excavation of the Irish elk, today still the pride of the Manx Museum's natural history display, in progress at Close-y-Garey, which was subsidised by a British Association grant.

It was probably in 1898 that Moore produced a thirty-two page booklet of *The Letters of Lieutenant Edward Christian of Lewaigue, 1804-1809*, a young Manxman who had served in the Napoleonic Wars. It was the first of several pamphlets, usually undated, on small corners of Manx history. In October he paid another visit to Oxford, staying in the Master's Lodgings in Jesus College, now occupied by John Rhys. As ever, this was a stimulating experience. He met his friends the folklorists Laurence and Alice Gomme, and Ernest Bennett, a fellow of Hertford who had recently returned from the Sudan, where he had been at the battle of Omdurman as a war correspondent. He also met again Dr W. R. Morfill, 'the great authority on Slavonic languages', and Henry Bradley at the Clarendon Press – 'had a long talk with him about Manx history'.

In the spring of 1899, while on holiday in Bath, he called on Dr John Beddoe at his home near Bradford-on-Avon. In July he attended the National Eisteddfod held in Cardiff (Chapter 7). From these sparse references it might appear that after his burst of literary productivity during the years 1890 to 1896, Moore's energies were now wholly absorbed by Manx politics and his young family. Nothing could be further from the truth. He was about to publish his master work, the fruit of many years of research, reflection and writing. At the end of 1900 he recorded simply 'My History of the Isle of Man which was issued on the 1st of October has been remarkably well received by the Reviewers [his capital R], nearly all the leading English newspapers having given it lengthy and most favourable notices'.

A History of the Isle of Man, in two volumes with a combined length of over 1,000 pages, was published in London by T. Fisher Unwin. Nothing on this scale had ever before been written about Manx history, and the book remains the standard authority to which all subsequent historians must refer. It was reprinted twice in the latter part of the twentieth century, in 1977 by the Manx Museum and National Trust, and in 1992 by its successor, Manx National Heritage. The archives of the Isle of Man were not, at the time Moore wrote, as organised and accessible as they have since become. Perhaps they had at an earlier date been too accessible: when the Assistant Keeper of the recently-founded Public Record Office in London, W. H. Black, visited the Island in 1839, he reported, 'Nothing here can be found, and I am assured ... as no secret, that anything may be stolen or destroyed by any lawyer [or] clerk on the Island. There are no calendars, nor anything to prove what belongs to the Public'.[18] But Moore had considerable resources for his research. In 1891 he owned about 340 books and pamphlets relating to the Island.[19] As a member of the Island's ruling elite, he could easily gain informal access to repositories of official records, from parish records to the documents kept by the Clerk of the Rolls, and even to the Derby Papers at Knowsley. Those who may doubt the authenticity of his research have only to consult the acknowledgements in his preface, and the footnotes to the whole work.

Moore seems to have conceived the idea of a history of the Island during his year as President of the IoMNHAS: in his address as the retiring President at the annual meeting in Douglas in March 1893, he urged upon his audience that 'We need to cooperate to produce a comprehensive history of the Isle of Man'.[20] Perhaps no collaborators were forthcoming, so he later decided that he would have to write the history on his own.

The work is an enormous compendium of information. The first volume covers the Island's history from its earliest inhabitants to Revestment in 1765. The second volume continues the narrative to 1866, 'the renewal of home rule', i.e. the introduction of elections for the House of Keys. There are sections on 'The Recent History', 'Constitutional History', 'The Land Question and its Settlement' and 'The Three Great Industries' (agriculture, fishing and mining) followed by lists of kings, governors and bishops, sources and an index. As a conclusion to the book, the last sentence, 'A deposit of fuller's earth has just been discovered in Michael', could be said to be lacking in weight. But this dry factual approach is typical of what was required by John Seeley and his fellow examiners of candidates taking the History Tripos at Cambridge in the 1870s.

John Quine's judgement on Moore's historical work in general was that he showed 'real energy, fixedness of purpose, and acute conscientiousness', but possessed no style in his writing. 'To make the past, or any epoch or incident of it, march again was for him quite impossible. But, if for that reason somewhat lacking in charm, his historical work by virtue of the sterling quality of conscientiousness is and will remain invaluable'. Quine's comments on Moore's *A History of the Isle of Man* largely repeat this: the work was 'his most important literary effort. Though wholly without any imaginative qualities or grace of style he ... had a comprehensive view of his subject. To this volume one turns as to the standard work of reference, but one does not read it for any pleasure in the perusal'.

This is a harsh, but perhaps a just assessment. Moore was certainly no Gibbon, Macaulay, Carlyle or Trevelyan, and did not aspire to be that kind of literary historian. But his book has one substantial merit, in the view of this reader, on which Quine fails to comment. At the time when so many historians restricted themselves solely to political history, Moore produced a work which included a good deal of social and economic content, focused on the condition of the Manx people. And he nailed his colours to the mast as a progressive liberal, asserting that 'It is no exaggeration to say that the

Manx people have made greater progress in all that appertains to civilization since 1866 than during the whole of the hundred years preceding that date'.[21] This was not, perhaps, a perspective which Quine shared.

Moore followed his *History* with two further books, both published in September 1901. *The Story of the Isle of Man: An Historical Reader for Manx Schools*, with illustrations, was published, like the *History*, by T. Fisher Unwin, and successfully condensed Manx history into a 150-page textbook for children. *Manx Worthies, or Biographies of Notable Manx Men and Women*, containing more than 150 brief biographies, was published by S. K. Broadbent with the support of subscribers. This had been a project of Moore's ever since the days of the *Manx Note Book* (1885-7), and he had mentioned it to T. E. Brown in 1895.[22] Now it came to fruition, and has ever since been one of his most popular books, being reprinted in 1929 and 1971. *New Manx Worthies*, published in 2006, is a work which brings Moore's lists up to date with entries from the last 100 years, emulating his original initiative.

In August 1901 he attended the Pan-Celtic Congress in Dublin (see Chapter 7) and in 1902 became occupied with royal occasions (Chapter 8). During 1902 he amused himself at odd moments by taking notes from old runs of insular newspapers and the diaries of Isabella Moore of Pulrose (1817-1850) and Paul Bridson (1841-1876), as a preliminary to his own notes from 1876 on, and the diary he started in 1885. He wrote, 'I do not flatter myself that these notes are likely to be of much interest to anyone. Having practically finished all the literary work I am likely to do, they will offer some relief for my inveterate habit of scribbling something!' He had completed his best-known works, but would continue to 'scribble something' for the rest of his life.

Chapter 6

POLITICIAN

It was almost inevitable that a man with Arthur Moore's intelligence, social standing and record of involvement in public affairs should enter the House of Keys. He was first asked to stand for Garff in 1883, but declined. In 1885 P. H. Leece, one of the MHKs for Middle, Moore's home sheading, became seriously ill, pressed Moore to succeed him, and died. A move to draft A. N. Laughton, High Bailiff of Peel, failed, and Moore's was the only hat in the ring. The *Examiner* protested that his views were unknown to the public, and that there ought to be a contest. 'A man may make a respectable churchwarden and be able to take weather observations pretty correctly, without having the necessary requirements of a good legislator'. But no other candidate appeared, and on 28 July, at the Douglas Courthouse, Arthur Moore was duly declared elected. Asked to make a statement, he said that he was both a landlord and a tenant, and that he and his father were the largest employers of labour on the Island. 'As for his views on political matters, it did not seem to him that there were any burning questions now before the country'. This was the politics of influence and status; it was not a promising start for a democratically elected politician.[1]

On 2 October Moore was sworn in both as a member of the House of Keys and as Captain of the Parish of Onchan, a position he held until 1895 when he resigned in an effort to reduce his public commitments. On 15 October he attended his first Tynwald Court. 'Harbour Works under discussion. Much talk but little result'. This was to be true of many of the debates he would sit through over the next twenty-four years. Far from the Isle of Man being a *Land of Home Rule* (the title of Governor Spencer Walpole's book), at this time the real power lay with the Governor, or in London. But his membership of the Keys did enable Arthur Moore to make a valuable contribution to decision-making and to public life in the Island.

For his first eighteen months in the Keys he was learning the ropes and considering his position on the issues of the day. He supported successive redistribution bills designed to give Douglas more members of the Keys in line with the increased urban population, and to reduce the numbers in some of the country districts, but as he was not a Douglas member he was not centrally involved in the issue. At this time he was, along with the majority of the Keys, against giving drink licences to lodging-houses, an issue which was to rumble on for many years. Spencer Walpole was an active Governor, like his predecessor Henry Loch, and he worked with Tynwald in driving forward many new projects. Thus the year 1880 saw work begin to extend the Victoria Pier in Douglas and to improve the harbour, the ceremonial opening of Ramsey's iron pier and of the Foxdale railway line, and the laying of the foundation stone for the first Noble's Hospital, paid for by Henry Bloom Noble (the building is now the Manx Museum). For all these developments Arthur Moore had a ringside seat. In an extended note in his diary he mused thoughtfully on the difference between the policies of Loch, who had pressed forward the development of the Island at a rate that could not be sustained indefinitely, and those of Walpole who, though criticised by the *Isle of Man Times* as autocratic and centralist, was keener on judicious retrenchment, consultation with Tynwald, and the development of local government. He reminded himself that 'The finances of the Island are controlled by the Auditor-General in London, an officer who has the right to take exception to any item in any expenditure which the Governor may sanction and disallow it'.[2]

Moore was already known as an antiquarian enthusiast, especially as the editor of the *Manx Note Book*. He was therefore a suitable person to be appointed to the Manx Museum and Ancient Monuments Trustees when that body was set up in June 1886. The aim of establishing a Manx Museum would not come to fruition a long time, but Castle Rushen served as a temporary museum from about 1900. The Douglas Town Commissioners, and after 1896 the Council, insisted that such a museum be in Douglas, but shortage of funds and of a suitable building delayed this for many years. Meanwhile, the most valuable work the Trustees could do was to identify and conserve the ancient monuments of the Island, and in particular negotiate with the local clergy to provide protection from the weather for the ancient Manx crosses. In this work Moore played an important part.[3]

The first general election of his time in the Keys, in March 1887, was one in which he played no part at all. He was on his honeymoon, but was again elected unopposed, with his colleagues as the sitting members for Middle Captain Richard Penketh and William Dalrymple, who apologised for his absence. Arthur Moore had now ceased to be a beginner and was, perhaps, being listened to seriously. In May he was sent on a deputation from the Keys to the Legislative Council to discuss with them the fate of two bills, on wild birds and burial. He also spoke forcefully in a Tynwald debate, condemning the continued use of Castle Rushen as a prison, which he knew through his work as a magistrate to be unsuitable. A motion calling for a new prison to be built was carried. In December he proposed an amendment in the Keys to the St Matthew's Grammar School and Chapel Bill. The details of this bill are unimportant, but the point is that his amendment was carried unanimously. He was a cautious, pragmatic, intelligent politician who carefully chose the issues on which he spoke.

Another long note in Moore's diary, this time on the Poor Relief Bill, preceded the passing into law of the Act. Over fifty years after the 1834 Poor Law in England and Wales, the Island's legislature, led by the Governor, recognised that voluntary effort could no longer keep up with the problem of poor relief. At first, districts could apply to be placed under the new Act, which in September Douglas and Ramsey promptly did, introducing a compulsory poor rate.

In April 1888 Moore was appointed to the Board of Education, a central body of five members of Tynwald and the Governor, whose powers were in practice limited by the multiplicity of local school boards, many of them keen to spend less, rather than more, money on education. However education was an issue to which he could bring knowledge and enthusiasm. The first contentious issue Moore was involved in was a local one, arising from a meeting of Braddan ratepayers, which he had chaired, calling for further school accommodation. As a result of this row Cronkbourne School was handed over to the Board of Education but later closed, despite Moore's loyal advocacy of his father's objections (Chapter 1). He was a strong supporter of the new Board Schools opened in Hanover Street, Douglas, in 1889 with 'an excellent speech on education by Governor Walpole'. He also enthusiastically endorsed the proposal made in December 1890 to build a higher grade school in Douglas, at which children could pursue their education beyond the elementary level.

One further issue with which Moore concerned himself was the arrangements for Tynwald Day. In 1890 he noted in his diary that 'the ladies stormed the hill and made such a noise that it was impossible to hear the laws promulgated!' In 1891, however, 'the proceedings on the hill, which had been carried out in accordance with my recommendations, were much more orderly than usual'. He was always concerned about the maintenance of good order, both public and private.

The 1891 election in Middle was conducted in a rather more democratic style than its predecessors. It was rumoured that F. G. Callow, an advocate and large landowner in Onchan parish, intended to stand against the sitting members. In the event Callow did not stand, but chaired the public meeting at Onchan Board School at which he was told that, had there been four vacancies, rather than three, the old members would gladly have had him on the ticket! Two public meetings were held at which the candidates, though unopposed, stated their views and took questions. Forty people attended a meeting at Braddan, 150 one at Onchan, in mid-April 1891, and Moore, along with the other candidates, addressed this small section of his electorate.

He supported the redistribution of seats in the Keys, and wanted to see more money made available for maintaining and improving the roads. On balance, he favoured the property qualification for membership of the Keys, though he wanted to lower the minimum value required. On the vexed question of drink, he wanted to keep the existing law on Sunday closing, allow short term licences in the summer, and have one licensing court for the whole Island, which would be a committee of Tynwald. He supported shorter parliaments, to last five rather than seven years. He would vote for the abolition of cess, the tax which supported the Church, though he warned that if the Church had less money to help the poor, there would have to be a compulsory Poor Law, on the rates, for the whole Island. He had an open mind about the abolition of school fees, and advocated waiting to see how it worked out in England. He thought there should be more emphasis on technical education: '... in my opinion, we teach in our schools too much theory and too little practice'. In answer to a question, he said that he supported equal rights for Nonconformists and everybody else. These were the views he held in 1891, and presumably his hearers found them broadly satisfactory.[4]

He could have added that the Redistribution Act which had become law in January, removing one seat each from the rural sheadings of Michael and Garff, and giving Douglas two more seats to bring its representation up to five members, was precisely what he had proposed a year earlier, in February 1890. The new prison in Victoria Road, opened in March 1891, was also a development which he had supported, though possibly one not especially popular with his constituents. The opening of the Douglas Marine Drive in July, by contrast, was generally welcomed.

At times Moore's cautious, gradualist approach to new legislation led him to oppose progressive measures. In 1881 the vote had been granted to men who owned or occupied property worth at least £4 a year, as well as single women and widows who owned such property, thus enfranchising about thirty per cent of the adult population. In November 1891 a further instalment of electoral reform was considered by the Keys, and Moore spoke against amendments which would give the vote to female occupiers and lodgers, arguing that these were important and serious proposals which deserved prolonged examination and calm deliberation – in a word, delay. The eventual House of Keys Election Act of 1892 extended the vote to single women and widows *occupying* property worth at least £4, and male lodgers in unfurnished property worth £10, per annum. This increased the electorate to just over forty per cent of the adult population, though there was no general election under the new arrangements until 1897. The same Act removed the property qualification for Keys membership: in future all men, apart from clergy and Government office holders, were eligible.[5]

The other burning issue of 1891-2 was free education. Moore supported the principle, but was dubious about some of the details of the Governor's bill, and proposed several successful amendments. In particular, he was concerned about how the free schooling would be paid for, and wanted to avoid any encroachment on highways funding. The Governor proposed to raised the necessary funds largely by increasing the tax on tobacco. Moore was mollified by the announcement of a highways improvement programme, including Whitebridge Hill, Onchan, as an early priority.

In March 1893 Moore discharged an important responsibility effectively: he took charge of a new education bill in the Keys, and on the 25th recorded in his diary 'Carry it through with nearly all the changes I wanted'. Later he was centrally involved in discussions with the Legislative Council where his brother-in-law George Ring, the Attorney-General, for many years chairman of the Douglas School Committee, was presumably a valuable ally. The Education Act of 1893 passed into law on 5 July. It was 'a long consolidating affair of some 136 clauses'. Its central feature was the substitution for 'elementary education' of the broader term 'public education'. In future post-elementary education would no longer be the preserve of the independent sector alone. It was a first move towards what would ultimately become the norm of secondary education for all. No children under the age of thirteen were to be employed during school hours, and the school-leaving age was raised to fourteen. This was an Act of which Arthur Moore had reason to feel proud. The details of the Acts passed by Tynwald do not, perhaps, make riveting reading, but they vitally affected the lives of most Manx people.[6]

On 15 November Moore voted against a further electoral reform bill. Again, he thought the time was not ripe. It was too soon to go further with reform and redistribution; the House should keep a close eye on the changing population statistics, wait and see. Furthermore, there was no demand for it in the country. In 1893, he may well have been right about that. The bill was thrown out by twelve votes to ten.

In the same month, Governor Walpole was appointed as Secretary to the

Post Office, and left the Island. 'His administrative talent and his aptitude in finance have been invaluable', wrote Moore in his diary. In addition, he had shared and supported Arthur Moore's scholarly and historical interests, and Moore and Louisa had often been guests at his table. Walpole had been Governor for eleven years and, as the farewell address from the House of Keys stated, 'During your tenure of office the doors of the [Legislative] Council Chamber have been opened to the public, the representation of the people amended, and the protection of the ballot extended to the electors. Free Education has been granted and provision, where required, for the maintenance of the poor. Public buildings have also been erected for the accommodation of the Legislature, the preservation of our national records, the safe custody of prisoners and the shelter of the poor. Extensive harbour works have been constructed... The finances of the Island have been placed on a satisfactory basis and municipal government developed and encouraged'. Over the previous six years, Arthur Moore had helped to implement these reforms.

The new Governor, Sir West Ridgeway, arrived in December. He had spent twenty-six years as a soldier and civil servant in India, five years as Under-Secretary for Ireland, and then headed a diplomatic mission to the Sultan of Morocco.[7] Moore wrote in his diary: 'There was a great demonstration on the pier. I did not go down and did not meet him until a fortnight later on the golf ground. He appears to be a quiet and gentlemanly (but nervous and irritable) man, but there is doubtless a good deal of power behind an unassuming exterior'.[8] Ridgeway was extremely capable, but he only stayed in the Island for two years before his appointment as Governor of Ceylon.

During the first of these two years, Arthur Moore was not working at full strength; he was still grieving for his baby son. He recorded events such as the beginning of the Douglas Town Improvement Scheme, in effect slum clearance followed by the erection of 'workmen's dwellings' in new streets, and the opening of the electric tramway to Ramsey. He appreciated the facilities in the new Tynwald building, and selected the stained glass designed by the famous London firm of Clayton and Bell. But he did not avoid controversy altogether. In the first place, he changed his mind about liquor permits, and seconded the Governor's successful bill allowing boarding-house keepers to take out permits for the sale of beer and stout on their premises at certain times of day. But he caused more of a stir outside Tynwald by a speech he made to the Church's Diocesan Conference in October, as one of a number of clergy and laymen asked to state their views on Sunday observance. Moore started by outlining the history of the issue, saying that he thought the Manx a religious and observant people, but that with the growth of the visiting industry there was a movement towards a greater degree of freedom. There were scarcely any boats or trams on a Sunday, and public houses were only open to bona fide travellers, but there were Sunday concerts, and carriage excursions. He recommended the open air services at Braddan and Douglas Head, but thought that there was no harm in visitors enjoying concerts, excursions, or indeed museums and picture galleries if such were available, especially as many of the working-class visitors from smoky industrial towns were only in the Island for a long weekend. He was in favour of reasonable recreation for the working classes: 'Sunday should be a day of cheerful recreation of spirit, a day which should bring the opportunity of mental and moral elevation; it should not be a day of penal gloom, to be anticipated with repugnance and endured with reluctance'. Clearly these opinions were anathema to many of the clergy. John Quine wrote that Moore had caused a sensation with his liberal views.[9]

In 1895 Moore was back in form as an active participant in Tynwald debates. He spoke again on licensing issues, steered a Church Bill (involving the creation of a cathedral chapter of canons on the Island) through the Keys, and presented his own Promulgation Bill to simplify the presentation of new laws on Tynwald Day, which became law in January 1896. He continued to agitate for the improvement of the road up Whitebridge Hill, which was subject to endless delay.[10] He devoted one of his long diary notes in May to the growth of Douglas and its municipal incorporation as a borough council. The year also saw the introduction of a Douglas telephone service, and the completion of the Snaefell Mountain Railway. Commenting in his diary on the Governor's appointment to Ceylon, he wrote in September: 'I am very sorry that he is leaving. He is a sharp, clever, capable man, with an intuitive knowledge of managing men. He has been especially kind to me'. This probably refers to Ridgeway's compassionate attitude to Moore's family difficulties and losses, as well as several good dinners at Government House. Ridgeway did what he could to speed up legislation and complete any unfinished business before he left the Island, but even so there was probably some resentment at his departure after so short a time as Governor. If so, it was not shared by the Moores. Arthur had abandoned his initial reservations, and in November he recorded that 'We have sent Governor and Lady Ridgeway a present – a silver fruit dish – on our own account instead of joining in the ladies' testimonial to Lady R. The Governor has been so specially kind to me that I wanted to include him'.

The new Governor was Lord Henniker, formerly a Conservative MP (1868-74), a courtier and lord-in-waiting to Queen Victoria at various times from 1877 on, a substantial Suffolk landowner and the chairman of Suffolk County Council. Moore first met him in May 1896: 'As I proposed raising a debate on the governor's Financial Statements I had several interviews with him and found him most pleasant and friendly, but he is not, I imagine, brilliant'. This was a polite understatement. Coming after three dynamic predecessors – Loch, Walpole, Ridgeway – all of whom Moore had known or worked with, Henniker was the first Governor for many years who was not up to the job. Moore responded by taking a much more critical, even oppositionist, tone than he had ever previously done. He congratulated the Governor on his first budget, speaking in Tynwald on 13 May 1896, but then went on to attack its deficiencies and to claim that further consideration was needed of the financial statement for 1896-7. In the summer he gave his longest speech in Tynwald, ranging widely over financial policy for forty-five minutes, and thought the speech was well received.[11] He believed there needed to be proper financial scrutiny of the cost of the Queen's Pier, Ramsey, and that general revenue should be increased and expenditure reduced. He recommended suspension of loan interest payments, that provision should be made for an insular museum, and that the Island should administer its own Post Office, and borrow money for a longer period. He would probably never have made such a long and detailed speech, had he had confidence in the ability and competence of the man in charge of the Island's finances – Lord Henniker.

In January 1897 the House of Keys rejected a new Boarding House or 'Permit' Bill by seventeen votes to seven, a course which Moore supported: he argued that it was wrong to give out 800 more licences just before a probable general election. Lord Henniker dissolved the House of Keys and called the election because of the Keys' decision, and this was always known as the 'Permit' Election. The central election issue was licensing, with rural Methodist temperance advocates lined up on one side, and those involved in the tourism and entertainment industry, mainly in Douglas, on the other. During the 1890s a greater degree of public participation in politics, and pressure from below on politicians, was beginning to emerge. The Island's small but growing trade union movement, and the existence of the Manx Socialist Society, founded in 1895, were among the manifestations of a changing public mood.

This mood showed itself in Moore's constituency, which experienced its first contested election for twenty-seven years. First, a public meeting of electors, but without the old members of the Keys, was held at the Cooil School on 23 January, with R. J. Clague, a Douglas seed merchant, in the chair; thirty or more people were there to voice their discontents. The meeting raised a number of questions; most people there wanted to see a broadly liberal reformist programme, including reform of the land laws, an end to the permits, and to the cess law. The most trenchant speech came from Tom Cormode, the radical, Primitive Methodist, teetotal blacksmith from Quine's Hill, who in 1903 would become the first working man to enter the House of Keys. Cormode claimed that 'Middle Sheading has the reputation of being the most lifeless in the Isle of Man', and said he hoped to make it as alert as anywhere else. He thought it was a bad thing to select candidates before their programme was made public. He complained that the three old members often voted against each other, and that in practice the electors were represented by only one of their members (presumably the energetic Arthur Moore).

The *Examiner* commented, 'This sheading is now fully awake'. The old members were all in support of the Permits Bill, it claimed, and they would be opposed by R. J. Clague and F. G. Callow. Moore, the youngest of the three former members, now had to face the electorate on his own at three public meetings, since his allies Captain Penketh and Dalrymple Maitland were both too ill, or said they were. Arthur Moore rose to the challenge: in Braddan on 1 February, with George Drinkwater in the chair, he said that he was in favour of household suffrage but not yet manhood suffrage, that he supported the Ballot Act, and was against tea duties, death duties and income tax, the worst of all taxes. He came under fire for a vote he had given in the licensing court in favour of the Woodbourne Hotel, Douglas, which he argued was nothing to do with this election. The meeting, on a show of hands, was divided about equally for and against the old members.

At the meeting held in Onchan the next night, Moore enlarged on the achievements of the previous six years, since the election of 1891: a larger electorate, free education, and parish councils. The permit system was, and should remain, restricted to large boarding-houses. He was opposed to payment of MHKs, but in favour of travelling expenses. He would continue to press for expenditure on Whitebridge Hill, and, in answer to Tom Cormode, thought that Nonconformists should be able to use mortuary chapels. On a show of hands he had far more support than his absent colleagues: Moore 43, Maitland 17, Penketh 13. The last meeting, at Santon, the most rural and the furthest from Douglas, passed a resolution supporting all three of the old members. Shortly afterwards Callow retired from the contest, claiming that he did not wish to take advantage of the illness of two of his opponents, but Clague persevered, presenting himself as the farmers' friend, an opponent of permits, of the cess law, and of compulsory churchwarden service.

Election day, 9 February, saw a spirited contest, with election workers competing to get their supporters to the poll. The result was Moore 390. Maitland 385, Penketh 346, Clague 283, Callow (withdrawn) 11. Arthur Moore spoke to the crowd from the window of Douglas Courthouse after the result was announced. It was to be the only occasion on which he had to fight a contested election.[12]

In March there was a lengthy debate on the permit question and the House of Keys was split 12-12, which meant the rejection of the Permit Bill and no extension of the legislation. Moore continued to be a vigilant critic of the Governor's financial statement, demanding more time to study it thoroughly in 1897, and in 1898 successfully moving the statement to a Finance Committee which had not met since 1870. 'We have been too apt to leave things to the Governor', he said, and the committee suggested better arrangements for borrowing extra money. During 1897 and 1898 he continued to be the leading spokesman in the Keys on educational issues, piloting through the House the education estimates and an Education (Amendment) Bill in 1898. He continued to press the Highways Board to take more effective action on road improvements. He chaired the Keys committee which considered the details of the bill to abolish compulsory Church rates. He shared the general mood of frustration when, for the first time in thirty years, the Governor had not got any new laws ready to be promulgated on Tynwald Day, and an extra Tynwald Day had to be held a month later for that purpose. His diaries for 1897-8 have few references to politics, and the reader wonders if, resigned to Henniker's incompetence, Moore had become more centrally involved with his young family, the Golden Jubilee, his travels and above all his big book on Manx history, never mentioned but requiring constant hard work.

All this changed at the end of 1898 with the death on 9 November of Sir John Goldie-Taubman of the Nunnery, Speaker for the previous thirty-one years, the whole lifetime of the House of Keys as an elected body. Moore mused: 'There seems to be a good deal of feeling in favour of making me Speaker, but whether I shall get it or not, I cannot say. It is certainly an office that I should like. There were articles in my favour, both in the *Examiner* and *Sun* of the 19th'. On 9 December the Keys met in private session to elect a new Speaker, and according to press accounts, Arthur Moore was elected unanimously. 'I was very glad when it was all over. The insular Press has been practically unanimous in my favour and the most laudatory articles have appeared in it'.

But the election was not as straightforward as this account suggests. As Moore admitted in his diary, 'Mr Mylrea and I as the two candidates were asked ... to retire and we spent a rather trying half-hour together, keeping up a friendly chat the whole time. Then Mr Maitland came in and announced that I had been elected by 11 votes to 10! It was arranged that the election should appear to be unanimous publicly and so Mr Mylrea in a most kind and graceful speech proposed me and John Crellin, who had been my first proposer, seconded me. I then made a few remarks thanking the House and saying that I would try to perform my duties with the utmost impartiality'. The Manx public were deceived in order to maintain the fiction that the Keys were united, rather than split down the middle.

Yet this, too, was not the whole story, if the recently discovered account by John Quine is to be believed. Arthur Moore met his first biographer, the Revd John Quine (1857-1940) in the 1880s, through the Church and through shared antiquarian interests. Quine was a frequent contributor to the *Manx Note Book*. He is first mentioned in Moore's diary in December 1887 when, after the death of Parson Drury, 'Mr Quine took the service at Braddan and Cronkbourne. He has been licensed for 3 weeks'. In April 1897 Quine presented Moore with a copy of his novel *The Captain of the Parish*, of which both Moore and T. E. Brown thought highly. Perhaps as a result of this, the acquaintance became a friend. During the diocesan conference in October, Quine was one of several clergy invited to lunch at Woodbourne House. An ex-pupil of King William's College, and a graduate of Merton College, Oxford, Quine had been successively a curate at Kirk Michael, the Bishop's chaplain, and head of the Douglas Grammar School, a small private establishment with forty to fifty boys, from 1883 to 1895. He then became the Vicar of Lonan, a position he held for the next forty-five years. Thus by education and occupation, John Quine was a member of the gentlemanly class in the Isle of Man.

But he was dogged by poverty for most of his life. Born the son of a miller, and suffering from a sense of grievance from his infancy, his educational and social ascent via Peel Grammar School, King William's College and Oxford had not been easy. He had eleven children and while Vicar of Lonan relied on rabbit-shooting and fishing to feed them all. This was a world apart from the comfortable prosperity enjoyed by Arthur Moore. Quine had a reputation as a difficult, unclubbable man, and indeed, as his private writings especially reveal, he had a dark, resentful side to his character. Even reading between the lines of his preface to *Nessy Heywood*, it seems clear that he was envious of Moore and thought that if he had had the same advantages in life, he could have been a better historian and writer than Moore was.[13]

Quine's account, 'How Arthur Moore got to be Speaker of the House of

Keys', was written in the same notebook as his notes on Moore's diaries, but probably some time later than the events it describes; he writes 'December 1899' when he means 1898, and cannot remember whether Moore was elected by a majority of one or two votes. According to Quine, Moore called at Lonan Vicarage, anxious to see him, and left a message with Mrs Quine asking him to come to lunch at Woodbourne House, after which the following conversation ensued:

> 'Quine – You wished to see me, I suppose about the Speakership.
> Mrs Moore – Oh yes! (brimful eagerness) Who will get it?
> Quine – As things stand, not you, Mr Moore.
> Both Moores – Why??? (Mrs Moore more visibly eager; he equally, no question)'.

Quine explained that there were at that time three candidates – Moore, Mylrea and Joughin – and that if individual preferences were counted up, Mylrea would win, with Joughin and Moore splitting the opposition to him. 'I should say the two were on their beam-ends: and I rather enjoyed the sight of these utterly worldly little worldlings in the gall of chagrin, especially the wife!' The point was, Quine argued, that Joughin, who had no hope of winning, must be dissuaded from standing.

'My reason was that Mylrea was a cad, a conceited mongrel, only son of a sly, slimy Methodist bookseller who had made £20,000 by the monopoly of the bookselling trade, and the son brought up to be a far less scrupulous person, little affected bully and atrociously pretentious antlet. Not that I cared much for Moore, cast in too small a mould of manhood, selfish from a socially clever pitiless merciless mother, but according to relative worth, much better than Mylrea!!! It was to please myself, not Moore, that I decided to intervene!' Quine apparently had a visceral hatred of 'these cursed Methodists, with their hypocrisies and worldliness, their jealousies inter se'.

Quine set off to see his 'ass of an elder brother' at the Nunnery mill house, and more especially his brother's wife, who was a Methodist but hated Mylrea. He persuaded them to go and see his father, William Quine MHK, at Silverdale, and other supporters of Joughin, to show them why he must not stand. Joughin dropped out, Moore was elected by one vote, and a week or so later George Ring stopped Quine in Athol Street, asked him into his office, 'and made some gushing remarks about the excellence of the calculation I had made'.

There is no reason to doubt the truth of this story, even if Quine exaggerated the importance of his intervention. It gives a rare insight into the manoeuvring and jockeying for position which is an inevitable feature of political life, in the Isle of Man as elsewhere, and the episode certainly does not show John Quine in an attractive light. Two other aspects of the incident are worth pondering. First, why did Moore need Quine to assess the state of opinion in the House of Keys on his behalf? Was he himself, though a practised judge of men, set apart on such a social pinnacle that he could not mix freely with the other members of the Keys and find out their opinions? It is easier, admittedly, to find someone else to press one's case than openly to do it oneself. Secondly, the story seems to illustrate the importance of the fundamental religious, political and cultural division in Manx society, still potent at the end of the Victorian era, between the Church of England and the Nonconformists, and especially the Methodists. In an island without political parties, this division was perhaps equivalent to, or even stronger than, the antagonism between the Conservatives and Liberals in England. Moore, a conciliatory liberal, wanted to bridge this gap; Quine did not.

Arthur Moore was now Speaker of the House of Keys and, in the absence of parties, the acknowledged leader of the elected part of the Manx government. He was a man of very strong loyalties, and it is worth quoting a sentence from his speech of acceptance that he did not include in his diary. 'I shall maintain the traditions, rights and privileges of the ancient House of Keys with zeal and diligence, and I hope to justify your confidence'.[14] He soon showed his mettle. At the first meeting of the Keys over which he presided, on 13 January 1899, he felt that he had not been very successful. 'I had an awkward question to deal with and a difficult Bill, the abolition of Church cess'. But at his first Tynwald court as Speaker, on 24 January, 'I had cause to stand up for the Keys which, as I was new to the work, was somewhat embarrassing. The Governor put an amendment in accordance with the usual English parliamentary method, and I in putting it to the Keys did so in the way we are accustomed to. This was objected to by the Attorney-General [George Ring] and other members of the Council, but I stuck to my point and they had to give way'. It was a procedural point only, but an early sign of Arthur Moore's determination to uphold the rights of the House of Keys.

As Speaker, Moore was now frequently in demand on all sides, and approached by outside bodies to appear on behalf of the Keys, but played a less active role in Keys debates which he had, of course, both to attend and chair. He was under more pressure than ever before, and probably had less time to record his activities in his diary. Some things did not change: the Keys discussed licensing again and 'local option', and 'as a decent method of burying the question' passed it on to a committee of Tynwald. Three years later, in January 1902, the Keys were still having 'futile conferences with the Legislative Council about the Licensing Bill'.

Arthur Moore enjoyed the ceremonial part of his role, and turned up on Tynwald Day in 1899 in 'Diplomatic Court Dress', but was powerless to do anything about the absence of new laws for the second year running. This again necessitated a further Tynwald meeting at St Johns on 20 July to promulgate the new laws. He was invited to assume new business responsibilities, no doubt in part, at least, because he was Speaker. In April 1899 he was unanimously elected as a director of the Isle of Man Bank. 'Those who have congratulated me for the most part say that I ought to have been elected many years ago and I am inclined to agree with them'. In February 1900 he accepted, 'after much hesitation', a seat on the board of the Isle of Man Steam Packet Company.

Some of the things he was asked to do were of a less 'establishment' character. On 15 March 1899, 'I presided over a meeting of the United Debating Societies which lasted from 2.30 to 10p.m. with an interval for tea! After formal business and a discussion in the afternoon on the desirability of reviving the Manx language, '"Needed Manx Reforms" were considered in the evening. Some of the debaters showed considerable ability'. On 24 October he read a paper on the Constitution of the Isle of Man, which was well received, to the Douglas Progressive Debating Society. The debating societies which flourished around the turn of the century, assisted and encouraged by S. K. Broadbent, editor and proprietor of the *Isle of Man Examiner*, were one aspect of the new mood for reform, social and political discussion, and progressive change in the Island.

A major imperial issue which impinged on the Isle of Man, and divided opinion, was the Boer War (1899-1902). Moore probably kept his opinions mainly to himself, but his diary entries show that he lacked enthusiasm for the war. On 16 December 1899 there was 'a great celebration in Douglas for the War Fund' involving a parade through the streets in the afternoon, and in the evening a patriotic concert at the Palace. 'Considering how we have fared in the War so far, I think that the old-fashioned Day of Humiliation [a reference to the Crimean War of his infancy] would have been more in place'. John Quine in his preface to *Nessy Heywood* could not refrain from commenting, 'To the best of his friends it was possible for him to be exasperating when he said things of this sort'. Moore returned to this subject in January 1900, enumerating several families he knew who had had members killed, imprisoned or besieged in South Africa. 'Such is the way in which this wretched war affects most people, though in many cases more intimately'. In May, 'The Relief of Mafeking was celebrated with, for Manxmen, wonderful excitement and fervour. A crowd came at about midnight shouting singing and cheering and demanded a speech from the Speaker.

A. W. Moore as Speaker leaving St Johns Church on Tynwald Day 1899, in his 'Diplomatic Court Dress'. He is flanked by his fellow Middle MHKs William Arthur Hutchinson and Dalrymple Maitland (who would succeed him on his death). This is one of a collection of more than 20,000 photographs taken around Britain by Sir J. Benjamin Stone MP, for his National Photographic Record.

However I did not turn out and I heard afterwards that a young plumber had personated me and made an excellent speech with which the crowd was so pleased that they separated after giving three cheers for the Speaker and Mrs. Moore'. A more demagogic politician might have jumped at the chance to speak at a popular demonstration, but it is hard to imagine Arthur Moore doing that.

In the twentieth century the Keys had to consider issues which were new to the Isle of Man. These included an Employers' Liability Bill in 1901 and a Married Women's Property Bill in 1902, though neither was passed into law at that time. On Employers' Liability, the debate in the Keys on the Bill's second reading was presented with a petition signed by 887 working men, and they heard evidence both from employers and from representatives of the Douglas Trades and Labour Council. This was a new kind of politics. Another straw in the wind was the election of Hall Caine as MHK for Ramsey in a by-election in October 1901, on a radical programme with 458 votes as against 191 for P. M. C. Kermode. Moore was not pleased: 'He has avowedly been elected as an advertisement! His election speech was 'high-falutin" and impractical to the last degree!' Hall Caine turned out to be a very frequent absentee from the Keys chamber.

Lord Henniker was increasingly enfeebled, and undermined by family tragedies. In March 1901 his eldest son died from pneumonia, and in June one of his daughters, twenty-five year old Cicely, also died, from 'galloping consumption'. A year later, in June 1902, the Governor himself died, and his funeral was held on the Island before his coffined corpse was taken back to Suffolk for burial. Moore, who rushed back from London for the funeral, was not surprised. Expressing a trenchant opinion in his diary for once, he wrote 'Lord Henniker has been an utter failure as Governor. No doubt as a result of disease his mind became feebler and feebler till at last his memory almost entirely failed. Personally he was a kindly courteous gentleman and my relations with him have been of the friendliest nature'. An efficient and successful Tynwald Day followed a week later, arranged by a committee, 'but the whole thing was practically done by me'. Six weeks later, on 15 August: 'Announcement that Lord Raglan, grandson of the Commander-in-Chief in the Crimea, is to be our new Governor. For all that I can learn we are very fortunate'. That was what he thought at the time.

Chapter 7
CELTICIST

Arthur Moore's writings were part of a 'Manx renaissance' which both provided the intellectual foundations of twentieth-century Manx nationalism and were part of a wider 'Celtic renaissance' which involved enthusiasts in Ireland, Wales, Scotland, Brittany and Cornwall. A recent article by John Belchem gives Moore pride of place among 'an impressive cohort of poets, writers and cultural leaders' who constructed a Celtic identity and ethnicity for the Isle of Man.[1] Moore's 'Celticism' was expressed not only in his books and articles, but also through his participation in the Celtic movements of his day from 1899 onwards.

As a young man, Moore learned the Manx language from his godfather, 'Parson' Drury, Vicar of Braddan, who was renowned for his Manx Gaelic sermons, and who died in 1887. One of Moore's earliest publications was the first known historical sketch of the language, a paper given to the IoMNHAS in May 1887, and published both in *Yn Lioar Manninagh* and in the *Transactions of the Celtic Society of Montreal*.[2] His enthusiasm for Manx Gaelic was apparent in most of the books he wrote or edited in the 1890s, and was an essential part of his achievement. Without his knowledge of the Manx language, not only the translations of Manx carvals and Bishop Phillips' Prayer Book would have been impossible, but also the books on Manx names, folklore, ballads and music.

Language is a powerful expression of nationality, and enthusiasm for the study of Manx Gaelic has often, perhaps usually, been associated with enthusiasm for the idea of a Manx-Celtic national identity for the Island.[3] Moore shared and, indeed, helped to form this view, though he was not a strident propagandist.

In his research on local names (page 74), he had concluded that sixty to seventy per cent of Manx place-names were of Irish-Gaelic origin, twenty per cent Scandinavian and the rest English.[4] In his book on Manx folklore he stated on the first page his belief that 'the Island was so intimately associated with Ireland till the coming of the Northmen that it is not likely that it would have any early myths distinct from those in Ireland'.[5] In his collection of *Manx Ballads and Music*, Moore adhered closely to traditional Gaelic music and songs. In his study, with John Beddoe, of racial groups in the Island, he found a preponderance of people of Celtic descent almost everywhere except in the mainly Scandinavian north-western parishes of Jurby, Ballaugh and Michael.[6]

Moore's most impressive book, *A History of the Isle of Man*, had less of a Celtic emphasis, however, since it covered the whole chronological span of the Island's history up to the end of the nineteenth century. Within this, Chapter II, 'Celtic Period', occupies less than forty pages, and begins with the admission 'It might reasonably be contended that the Celtic period in Man ... belongs to the domain of myth and legend'.[7]

All Moore's 'Celtic' books were written in the 1890s, and preceded his involvement in the actual Celtic revival movement of his own day. Arthur Moore has often been described as 'the founder of the Manx Language Society'. The annual reports of the Society (which had become known as Yn Cheshaght Gailckagh, or the Manx Society) carried on their front page the rubric, in small print, 'Founded in 1899 by the late Speaker Moore' from 1916 on, at least until the 1950s and perhaps for longer, testimony to his enduring reputation. The latest repetition of this is in the entry on Moore in the *Oxford Dictionary of National Biography* (2004).

Sophia Morrison originally made the claim in her obituary of Arthur Moore, whom she admired greatly, but a few years later, in her article on 'The Origins of the Manx Language Society', she was more circumspect.[8] She recalled the origin of the language revival movement in the Peel Manx Language Association, founded during the winter of 1897-8, and the classes which soon began to flourish not only in Peel, but in other parts of the Island. She recollected that Moore had joined the Pan-Celtic Association, based in Dublin, 'about this time', and that its secretary, the Breton Edmund Fournier d'Albe, came to the Island in March 1899 when Moore chaired the inaugural meeting of the Manx Language Society.

William Cubbon, in a fiftieth anniversary lecture delivered in 1949, started with the usual claim that Moore had founded the Society, but went on to qualify this, talking of 'Speaker A. W. Moore's influence'. 'We found in 1898 that Mr A. W. Moore, Speaker of the Keys, one of the busiest of men, had been observing the movement with pleasure, and in a conversation that I had with him in the autumn of 1898, he said that the time had come to consider forming a central organising body. It was known that there was a definite proposal to hold a great pan-Celtic Congress in Dublin in the year 1901 and it would be fitting that a Manx Language Society should be formed to organise the Manx side of the affair'. Cubbon's memory of this conversation, fifty years later, may be correct, but in the autumn of 1898 Moore had not yet been elected as Speaker.

According to Cubbon, he himself sent out the necessary notices to the press, acted temporarily as secretary and wrote to a selected number of interested people. 'Through Mrs Laughton, secretary of the Fine Arts and Industrial Guild, a meeting was arranged to be held on one of the four days of the Guild festival, namely the 22nd March 1899. Speaker Moore presided over a large gathering composed of about seventy middle-aged and elderly men and women mainly from the Country Districts'.[9] The *Examiner* report of the meeting, reprinted as a pamphlet, tells us that the afternoon venue was the drawing room of Empire House, Queen's Promenade, Douglas, and counts the attendance as fifty.[10] Sophia Morrison's article listed the promoters of the meeting as A. W. Moore, Deemster Gill, John Crellin MHK, Dr John Clague, and the committee of the Fine Arts and Industrial Guild.

In short, it appears that quite a number of people were involved in the foundation of the Manx Language Society, and that it is misleading to describe Moore as the sole 'founder'. He may, as Cubbon suggests, have had the original idea; he chaired the inaugural meeting, and was elected as the first President. But he certainly did not do the work of organising and enthusing others, necessary to launch the new Society. He was still finding his feet, after only three months in the job, as Speaker of the House of Keys. This was, perhaps even more than his impressive Manx scholarship, the reason why he was lionised by the members of the Language Society. To have the holder of the most prestigious office in the Manx legislature as the figurehead of the new organisation was a coup, and a major advantage in publicising the Society and its work.

Moore's first recorded duty as President of the Society was to attend the Welsh National Eisteddfod in Cardiff in July, to which he was invited both in his official capacity, and in recognition of his great services to Manx literature. Interpretation of Arthur Moore's reactions to this event, and the later Celtic Congresses, is not straightforward because he recorded three out of four of these meetings in his missing travel diaries, so what we know comes down to us via the Revd John Quine's notes. They tell us in some detail that Moore arrived in Cardiff on 17 July, attended the Mayor's reception, and gave his speech as Manx delegate to Fournier d'Albe to read, presumably to check the content.

He stayed at St Fagan's Castle with Lord Windsor, who was both the President of the Eisteddfod and the Lord Lieutenant of Glamorgan, and met Sir Lawrence Alma Tadema and Hubert Von Herkomer, both artists whom he admired. The next day he took part in the Gorsedd procession, which set off at 8am. He could not understand the Archdruid, who spoke in Welsh, but he usually enjoyed ceremonial occasions, and described the Druids, in robes of white, the Bards, in robes of light blue, and the Artists in robes of light green. Von Herkomer presented a great sword which he had designed, and Lord Tredegar presented a golden horn. Moore also mentioned the Irish delegation, headed by Lord Castletown of Upper Ossory, the Highlanders, preceded by a piper, and the Bretons. All received decorations, but only Lord Windsor, Lord Castletown and Moore received the Druid decoration, a white ribbon round the arm, 'Agoriad Manaw', which he acknowledged and gave thanks for in his speech delivered in Manx. There followed the choral singing competition, 'uniting sounds of Wales and Brittany', before he returned to St Fagan's with Lord Windsor, the Breton Marquis de l'Estourbeillon, and Count Plunkett, Irish Home Ruler. Moore left Cardiff after lunch the next day, 19 July.

Quine's preface to *Nessy Heywood* adds the following observations: 'He seems, in his description of it, to acknowledge the whole affair to have been an amazingly stupid and puerile show. He had the good fortune to, at least, appear to take such things seriously; this arose from an idea he had of a duty to the Island, viz. that since there was this institution, the Island should at least be represented'. None of this appears in Quine's own notes on Moore's account of the Eisteddfod. Probably it was based on memories of a conversation between the two men. 'Amazingly stupid and puerile' and 'artificial and idiotic' sound like Quine's own opinions; the idea of a duty to represent the Island, whether at this event or at the Pan-Celtic Congress, could well have been something Moore said. An additional complication is that Quine was himself a member of the Manx Language Society, and attended its meetings from 1899 until about 1905. Presumably he had changed his mind about Celtic activities by the time he wrote the preface to *Nessy Heywood*. John Quine was an inconsistent man.

But Moore himself was not an entirely orthodox member of the Manx Language Society, or adherent of the Pan-Celtic cause. The first annual meeting of the Society, attended by some eighty members, was held at the Rosebery Hotel, Douglas, on 13 November, when Moore reported on his visit to Cardiff and on his year in office generally. That part of his presidential address in which he set out his belief that the Society should not confine itself to promoting the Manx language, but should also extend itself to study Manx history, music, ballads, carols, folklore, proverbs, place-names – on all of which he himself had written, 'in a word, to the preservation of everything distinctively Manx, and above all to the cultivation of a

A. W. Moore SHK, a vice-president of the Celtic Association, received the honorary degree of Druid 'in recognition of his splendid services to Manx literature' at the Welsh National Eisteddfod held in Cardiff in 1899. John Quine reported of a conversation with Moore about this event that, 'He seems, in his description of it, to acknowledge the whole affair to have been an amazingly stupid and puerile show', but there is nothing to indicate this in his notes on Moore's actual diary. Moore was at least spared the need to dress up in 'Druidic costume', which had first been seen at the Welsh National Eisteddfod held in Llandudno three years earlier.

national spirit', has often been repeated, notably in Sophia Morrison's 1914 article. But some other parts of Moore's address, which were not reprinted by Morrison, are much less well-known.

'Is it desirable to endeavour to revive the spoken Manx by teaching it to the young, or is it not? I venture to think that it is not'. He acknowledged that other people disagreed with him, but he thought that the language was only shared by a very limited number of people, and that practically it was of no value for gaining a livelihood. It would be better for young people to learn French or German. 'Much as I regret to think of the day when the grand and sonorous language of Ellan Vannin will be no more heard, yet I feel that I must prefer the practical to the sentimental and acquiesce in its disappearance'. It is an extraordinary irony that the man who would be remembered as the patron saint of Yn Cheshaght Gailckagh for the next half-century and more, was in fact opposed to the Society's main *raison d'être*.

He went on to recommend preserving a spirit of nationality, 'always provided that it contains no suspicion of disloyalty to the central authority. I need scarcely say that this condition is fulfilled in the Isle of Man, Her Gracious Majesty having no more loyal subjects than the Manx. Our loyalty to the Crown, as well as our separate nationality, is, it seems to me, admirably typified by our flag, combining as it does the Union Jack, with our own golden 'tre cassyn'. We are proud of being part of a mighty Empire, but we are proud also of being Manxmen. We are thoroughly English (using the word in its broadest sense) and yet we have a feeling that by our race, by our language, by our customs and traditions we largely belong to that gifted Celtic race which has played such a remarkable part in the history of the world. And yet, though more nearly allied to the Irish, the Scotch and the Welsh than the English, we are neither the one nor the other, but Manx.'[11]

Here Moore was on safer ground. The Manx Language Society and the Celtic Association, to which it was affiliated, were avowedly non-political bodies. Yet it may be doubted how many of their members, especially in Ireland, would have shared Moore's views, or been prepared to think of themselves as English, in any sense whatever. This rather tortuous statement explicitly expresses Moore's position, with his multiple allegiances – Manx, Celtic and English. It was the political philosophy in a nutshell of this particular Anglo-Manxman.

One other aspect of Moore's part in the foundation of the Manx Language Society is worthy of comment. Neither in 1898 or 1899, nor indeed subsequently, are there any references to the activities of the Society in Moore's diary, other than his visits to the Eisteddfod and the Celtic

Congresses in Dublin, Caernarvon and Edinburgh. He was a loyal member of the Society, but a figurehead. Busy man as he was, the impression given by this omission is that he was more necessary to the Society than the Society was to him.

In May 1900 a committee meeting was held at Woodbourne House, and Moore remained President until November, when he handed over to the Revd Ernest Savage. The Society had had a disappointing year, the secretary William Quayle reported, with no progress, no increase in membership, public interest at a low ebb, and almost all the Manx language classes having ceased to exist. There were only fifteen paid-up members, compared to twenty-six the year before. It must have looked as if the Manx Language Society would be a very short-lived phenomenon. Even the Pan-Celtic Congress, originally planned for 1900, had been postponed for a year due to the absence of the President, Lord Castletown, and 'the unsettled state of mind in the Celtic countries, occasioned by the South African war'. It sounded as though the organisers were worried by the possibility of arguments about the war disrupting the proper agenda of the Congress.[12]

Things improved in 1901. The year opened with the launch of *Celtia*, a Pan-Celtic monthly magazine, edited from Dublin by Fournier d'Albe. The first issue, in January, carried a message of welcome from Arthur Moore on behalf of the Manx Language Society, though he may not have been entirely in agreement with the magazine's statement that '*Celtia* will be the organ of militant Celticism, directed mainly against the deadening and demoralising influences of modern Anglo-Saxondom...' The magazine provided a focus for Celtic aspirations, but probably more important within the Isle of Man was the delegation, led by Moore, which persuaded the Governor, Lord Henniker, to include a question about language in the Island's 1901 census. The result, announced in June, was that 4,419 Manx resident (8.1 per cent of the total population), registered as Manx speakers, almost all of them bilingual, and most of them from the country districts. This was more than had been generally expected. But it did not include Arthur Moore himself, who told the census enumerator that he and all his household were English speakers. This was an accurate response: whatever Moore's skill in speaking the Manx language, as others of his class might perhaps be skilled in Latin or French, English was undoubtedly the language spoken in Woodbourne House.[13]

In August 1901, Moore, as Speaker of the House of Keys the senior Manxman in the Pan-Celtic movement, led the Manx delegation to the first Pan-Celtic Congress in Dublin. He had been elected as a vice-president of the Celtic Association in April, and was also now a vice-president of the

Manx Language Society. The Congress opened on Tuesday 20 August, when only two of the ten Manx delegates, Sophia Morrison and her friend Miss O. Joughin, both from Peel, had arrived, and walked in the opening procession. Arthur Moore arrived in Dublin on the 21st, and went to the ancient concert rooms in Great Brunswick Street where he met Lord Castletown, then to the Royal Hotel opposite the Kildare Street Club, where he met Professor Heinrich Zimmer. He next spent an hour at the Congress, perhaps listening to his compatriot William Quayle addressing the assembled delegates on the subject of Manx language and Manx music, before taking a stroll in Phoenix Park. He dined at the Club in the evening with Lord Castletown, the Hon. Stuart Erskine, a Scottish delegate, and Mr Campbell, Lord Castletown's secretary. On Thursday the 22nd, the third day of the Congress, he went to be photographed and then, at the request of Lord Castletown, chaired a session conducted by the Scottish activist Malcolm Macfarlane on the subject of Highland Gaelic music. Later that day there was a formal reception for the 'brothers from Manxland' who had been unable to be present at the opening ceremony: they included, in addition to Moore, John Crellin and William Quayle, J. J. Kneen, William Cubbon, the Revd W. Cooke, Henry Kelly of Port St Mary, and his son H. Percy Kelly. With the two ladies from Peel, the Manx delegation was ten strong, out of 100 delegates in all. The eight men joined Lord Castletown on the platform (the women perhaps being more reticent) and Moore made a speech in which he said that Manxmen considered Ireland as their motherland, with the same legends, traditions and history (this according to Fournier d'Albe, presumably the author of the report in *Celtia*). He was acclaimed as the Speaker of the only Celtic parliament.

On the fourth day, while William Cubbon and the Revd Cooke were doing their best to persuade the delegates that the next Congress should be held in the Isle of Man in 1902, Arthur Moore and John Crellin spent the morning sightseeing, before Moore went off to Howth Castle where he met, again, Lord Castletown and another Plunkett, the Right Hon. Sir Horace. They went on to a soirée held by the Dublin Literary Society, where he saw the German philologist Kuno Meyer, Professor Zimmer, and the poet and song-writer A. P. Graves (whose son Robert, later the famous author, was then six years old). The Congress may have lasted until Sunday the 25th, but on the Saturday Moore travelled down to County Cork with Lord Castletown, six Bretons and several other guests, to stay at Doneraile Court. He remained at Doneraile until Tuesday the 27th before returning, via Waterford and Kilkenny, for a visit to the Dublin Horse Show, and to catch the boat home on the 28th.[14]

Arthur Moore had always enjoyed high society, and he had probably become grander since being elected Speaker. The impression given is that he was an effective figurehead for the Manx delegation, but avoided most of the sessions of the Congress and preferred consorting with Lord Castletown and his fellow aristocrats and grandees. John Quine's inevitable gloss on the event, in his preface to *Nessy Heywood*, speculated 'if the Manx representative [Moore] had also been himself a Celt, the meeting would surely have betrayed him into tears and sentiment ... Arthur Moore, though not a Celt, was justified in being where he was ... among those enthusiasts of nature and disposition alien to his own'. Quine had himself been elected as a delegate to the Congress in 1900, but must have withdrawn.

By the end of 1901, although it had been decided that there was no prospect of holding a Pan-Celtic Congress in the Isle of Man in 1902 because the Island was still suffering from the aftermath of the Dumbell's Bank failure, the Manx Language Society was in better shape, assisted no doubt by the effect of the Congress in raising morale and the election of Sophia Morrison as the new secretary. A Manx choir sang at the Eisteddfod for the first time at Bangor in 1902.

Arthur Moore remained a vice-president of both the Celtic Association and the Manx Language Society, and attended meetings when he could. In August 1904, despite his reservations about the teaching of Manx, he acted as official examiner of teachers for the Board of Education, and reported that J. J. Kneen's paper was excellent and that he was competent to teach the language. If he had known the name of the candidate, wrote Moore, he would have said that he did not need to be examined.[15] His main contribution to the Society, however, was the role he played at the triennial Pan-Celtic Congresses. In late August and early September 1904 he again led a Manx delegation to the Congress, this time at Caernarvon. He was billeted with Sir William Preece at Penrhos Castle, where he arrived on 30 August before attending Lord Castletown's address to the Congress. On the 31st there was a reception for the delegates in the castle: this time the Manx contingent was some twenty-seven strong, including the editors of the *Examiner* and the *Manx Sun*, S. K. Broadbent and, at this time, William Cubbon. Many of the guests at the reception were dressed in Gaelic and Breton costumes. Arthur Moore was probably relieved that attempts to devise a Manx national costume had not come to fruition, and he appeared in his usual gentlemanly attire, complete with wing collar, waistcoat and watch-chain, and carrying a top hat and rolled umbrella – not at all Celtic. There was an evening concert of Celtic music.

On 1 September he was called upon unexpectedly to make a speech, and

A. W. Moore led a twenty-seven strong Manx delegation to the 'flamboyantly romantic'* Celtic Congress held in Caernarvon in 1904. Unlike most delegates from the other Celtic countries, who attended in 'traditional' costumes, the Manx delegation appeared in modern dress. This photograph was one of a collection taken at Caernarvon Castle by the notable Welsh photographer John Wickens.

* Marion Löffler, *'A Book of Mad Celts': John Wickens and the Celtic Congress of Caernarfon 1904*, Gomer 2000.

said he thought the Isle of Man was 'doing very well, considering the summer flood of Saxon trippers. He attributed much to the Home Rule they in the Manx Island possessed, and elicited much applause when he referred to his political dream, the same condition for all the Celtic nations, Home Rule for each, and an Imperial parliament to knit all together in one Empire'. Another report of his speech was slightly different: 'The best solution of existing problems in Parliament was to institute a general scheme of devolution or Home Rule all round. He hoped to see a truly Imperial parliament dealing solely with Imperial questions, and local assemblies for each nationality dealing with its distinctively home affairs'. Predictably, Quine could not resist referring to this in his notes as 'rot', and in his published version commented loftily, 'At these gatherings it really does not matter what anybody says: for, of course, people are not there to take or be taken seriously'. If this was 'rot', it was only so in one particular: the status of Brittany could hardly be settled by Home Rule within the British Empire. Otherwise, a century later Moore's scheme seems remarkably modern and prescient. He did not foresee Irish independence, but devolved 'Home Rule' now exists in Northern Ireland, Scotland and Wales, as well as in the Island, to various degrees.

Later Moore chaired a lecture on Celtic music, and went to a garden party hosted by the Lord Lieutenant of Caernarvon, where he met Sir Owen Roberts, chairman of the Clothworkers, and discussed the problems of education in Peel. On 2 September he drove to see a bilingual Latin and Ogham inscription. Rain prevented the last meeting of the Congress, and on the 3rd he travelled home. 'But, of course', according to Quine, 'he stood quite outside the enthusiasms'.[16]

On Tynwald Day in 1907, 'As none of the coroners were able to read Manx I was asked to do it by the Governor and promulgated the only Act which had received the Royal Assent i.e. the "Enquest of Deaths". I was greatly complimented on my pronunciation – nothing like it for 30 years!' The next year, 1908, he promulgated seventeen acts in Manx, and in 1909 eleven. In official circles, he was the best Manx speaker in the Island.

Moore's account of the 1907 Celtic Congress in Edinburgh is to be found in his main diary. It was very much the mixture as before. He stayed from 24-28 September at the Carlton Hotel, 'rather noisy but comfortable'. He was one of only three Manx delegates. He hob-nobbed with Lord Castletown, went to a reception hosted by the Lord Provost, was introduced to the Marquess of Bute and the Irish Home Rule nationalist politician Sir Thomas Esmonde and his wife. The outstanding feature of the Congress from a Manx viewpoint was the performance by a Manx male voice choir, consisting of Messrs Noah Moore, Taggart, Watterson and Longden. At the concert on the 26th, 'the Manx singing was certainly the most striking and original feature. I introduced them and said a few words about Manx music. They sang *Kirree fo Niaghtey* and *Mylecharaine* and as encores *Tappaghyn jiargey*, *Illiam Dhone* and *Mannin veg veen*. They had a most enthusiastic reception. Their singing was unaccompanied'. Moore knew Edinburgh well, so he did no sightseeing in the city, but took the train south to see Rosslyn Chapel before travelling home on the 28th.[17]

The Manx concert at Edinburgh makes an appropriate ending to this account of Arthur Moore's Celticism. He was, above all, a cultural, not a political, Celticist and Manx nationalist.

Moore's last two scholarly articles, which did not break new ground, were probably commissioned as a result of his Pan-Celtic activities. 'The Connexion between Scotland and Man', which appeared in the *Scottish Historical Review* in July 1906, recapitulated the mediaeval history of the link down to the fifteenth century, and asserted on its first page that 'Of the four countries adjacent to the Isle of Man Scotland is nearest, and has had perhaps the most intimate connexion with it'. 'The Connection of the Isle of Man with Ireland', which appeared in the *Celtic Review*, 15 October 1909, focused mainly on the years from the fifth to the eighth centuries, with a few remarks about later developments. 'The connection between the two countries has been a very intimate one'. Manx personal names were mainly closer to Irish ones, while the language, he thought, owing to the more recent connection with Scotland, approached somewhat more closely to Scots than to Irish Gaelic.

'Though Man now looks eastwards, rather than westwards, it has a remaining bond which still links it closely to Ireland, a bond that can never be broken – the bond of race'. A hundred years ago, historians habitually thought and wrote in such terms, and these two articles can be seen as affectionate salutes to two of the Island's three Celtic neighbours, rather than the expression of a deep Celtic racialism, in the modern sense.[18]

Chapter 8

ROYALIST

The magic of monarchy, not extinct even today, was perhaps at its most potent in Arthur Moore's lifetime. For him, enthusiasm for the British royal family was not at all inconsistent with his Celtic allegiances. In fact it was such a central part of his beliefs and attitudes that it cannot be omitted from his biography. His royalism was shared with millions of other people, and was perhaps taken for granted by the majority of British and Manx Victorians. In this he may be typical of his age, but while most royalists worshipped from afar, Moore had opportunities for closer access.

The announcement at a children's party at Kirby in 1861 of the death of Prince Albert, and a fête held to celebrate the marriage of the Prince of Wales in 1863, have already been mentioned as among Arthur's childhood memories. He recorded in his diary for 1869 the visit of Prince Arthur, Duke of Connaught and a son of Queen Victoria, to the Island. The prince dined at Government House, where Arthur's parents were introduced to him; Arthur himself told John Quine that he had 'a vague memory' in which he and the prince were dancing in the same quadrille. Arthur's participation in the Rugby School cadet corps must also have involved frequent expressions of loyalty to the Queen.

In 1871 W. F. Moore, as chairman of the Douglas Chamber of Commerce, visited the International Exhibition in London and was presented to the Prince of Wales. In 1872 Arthur himself attended the thanksgiving service at St Paul's for the prince's recovery from illness, and saw the queen and other members of the royal family. Such events had the cumulative effect of reinforcing and strengthening his admiration for the monarchy. After he left Rugby in 1872, and his father had left public life in 1875, there were fewer opportunities for close encounters with the royals until Arthur's own entry into the public arena.

Queen Victoria's Golden Jubilee in 1887 was the first major event held to celebrate the monarchy for many years. Early in February Arthur Moore, as Captain of the Parish, called a meeting in Onchan board school to consider ways of celebrating the Jubilee in the summer. The meeting decided that this should be done by providing free entertainment for the poor and for schoolchildren. On 29 June an official Jubilee Lunch was held in a large marquee at Government House, followed by a garden party. This was the way in which the Island's elite celebrated the event, and Arthur and Louisa Moore were there. The Onchan parish celebrations on 6 July seem to have been a mixed blessing: the sports in the afternoon were 'only moderately successful'. They were followed by a children's tea at 4.15pm, and a speech from Governor Walpole. The rain came on at five o'clock, so the proceedings were adjourned to the old parish school where Mrs Walpole judged a children's competition for wild flower bouquets. At six there was a tea for adults at the board school, with Louisa Moore in charge of one table. At eight o'clock there was a concert, including a speech by Arthur as Captain of the Parish. 'It did not come to an end until 10.20pm, by which time we were thoroughly tired out and thankful that the Jubilee was over!' This local manifestation of royalist fervour does not seem to have stirred him deeply, but of course there were no royal persons present.

Royal persons did not have to be British to cause Arthur Moore a flutter of excitement. In London exactly two years later, returning from a Gentlemen v. Players cricket match at the Oval on 6 July, 'On our way back over Vauxhall Bridge we had an excellent view of the Shah [of Persia]. The people had been turned off the Bridge, but we slipped on unobserved by a side approach and he passed within a few yards of us and bowed most politely!' The next day, a Sunday, evidently eager for a second look, they went to the Park, but due to rain 'we did not see much, just catching a glimpse of the Prince of Wales and the Shah'.

The Queen's Diamond Jubilee in 1897 was a much grander event than its 1887 predecessor, and Arthur Moore was pleased to learn on 1 June that he was one of the three members of the Keys fortunate enough to get a seat to watch the Jubilee procession in London. The Moore family turned up in force on 22 June, several of them being in London already. Louisa, Edith and Hannah Moore had secured a viewpoint at the *Punch* office in Fleet Street, Rosie and Mildred were in the Haymarket, while Arthur himself, as an invited dignitary, was on Constitution Hill. 'My seat was certainly one of the best in London', with views to Hyde Park Corner on one side and almost to Buckingham Palace on the other. Next to him were the rest of the official Manx delegation, Messrs Robert Stephen and W. M. Kerruish from the House of Keys, Deemster J. F. Gill and Sir James Gell, Attorney General.[1] Close by was one of Arthur's many cousins, Susan Emily Christian (the future Mrs Hicks Beach, whose evocative if sometimes inaccurate memories, *The Yesterdays Behind the Door*, would be published in 1956). The royal procession, starting at 9am, took several hours to pass, including in order colonial mounted troops, home troops, sailors, horse artillery and lancers, the Indian princes ('splendid and gorgeous creatures'), field-marshals and their aides-de-camp, foreign ambassadors and 'our own numerous Royal family', foreign princes and finally, 'H. M. the Queen looking well but sad'. It was all 'a magnificent and never to be forgotten sight'.

In the early afternoon Arthur went out alone in the crowds to see the decorations in Piccadilly, and after tea in the Strand and Fleet Street. He thought most of them were 'commonplace'. After dinner he took Rosie and Mildred out on foot to see the illuminations, although some were not working. In Piccadilly they were 'engaged by an enormous crowd and were helplessly carried along by it'. It was 'a good-natured, but decidedly odoriferous crowd', in the middle of which Arthur was surprised to see the Revd William Drury, eldest son of his godfather, 'in a very excited state waving his arms about over the heads of the crowd! He appeared to be threatening two policemen with summary vengeance for some misdeed!' Despite this entertaining and unexplained episode, Arthur found the illuminations 'on the whole disappointing'.

As usual, the Moores stayed in London for a few days and went to the theatre (Ellen Terry and Henry Irving again, in *Madame Sans-Gêne*, with Terry in the title role and Irving as Napoleon), and to the Royal Academy, where they saw the Grand Duke and Duchess of Hesse and Prince Sergei of Russia among their fellow-visitors. Arthur observed that 'The Duchess went about with the Prince and did not seem to be on good terms with her husband who is a very common looking individual'. They did the rounds of their relations, and Louisa had her photograph taken by Alice Hughes, the leading society photographer in London.[2]

But the Jubilee celebrations were not over, and on 25 June Arthur went off alone to Southampton to watch the Review of the Fleet the next day. He had a place booked on a 1,400-ton steamer, the *Lady Hudson-Kinahan*, owned by the British & Irish Steam Shipping Company, which cruised around the Royal Navy's array to give those on board a close view. The ironclad battleships were anchored in five lines, each about six miles long, with a sixth line of foreign warships including American, Russian and Italian vessels, and a seventh line of Britain's finest merchant steamers. Arthur was impressed by the wonderful spectacle, 'both from the point of view of its beauty, but still more from the astounding display of power'. The Prince of Wales reviewed the fleet, and was received with the appropriate salutes, in the afternoon. The food on the boat ran out, and there was a tremendous thunderstorm in the afternoon, but Arthur was astonished and delighted by the illumination of the fleet and accompanying fireworks from 9.30pm until midnight. 'A more wonderful and beautiful spectacle I certainly never saw'. The boat arrived back in Southampton at 4.30am, and he got to his hotel at about five, but the experience had been worth it. The only Jubilee event in the Island mentioned in his diary was the distribution of medals to Douglas schoolchildren by his brother-in-law George Ring, at the Palace Ballroom on 7 July.

On 19 June 1899 Arthur Moore was present at court at a levee, or royal reception, to mark his appointment as Speaker of the House of Keys six months earlier. We do not have his account of this, because it was in the travel diaries – tacked onto the end of his cycle tour in Brittany which had ended two days earlier. Quine's notes tell us only that Moore was presented by the Home Secretary to HRH, so this must have been his first meeting with the future King Edward VII.

As Speaker, Moore played a key role in the protocol of succession when Queen Victoria died on 22 January 1901. His own response was typical of very many of Victoria's subjects: 'A terrible shock indeed. We had all I think come to think that she was immortal'. On 30 January a meeting of Tynwald was held at St Johns in snow and bitter cold to proclaim Edward VII as the new king, and to vote an address to him, which Moore seconded on behalf of the Keys. A state service, with the church draped in purple, was held at St George's in Douglas on 2 February, the day of the queen's funeral.

The coronation of Edward VII followed in the summer of 1902. On 23 June Arthur and Louisa set off for London to stay with Frank and Cecilia Pearson and their three small daughters at 3 Langford Place, St John's Wood. The trains were very crowded, and the next day they heard the news of the king's serious illness and the postponement of the coronation. The Moores spent the day of the 25th following the route of the planned procession to see the decorations, which Arthur again found unimpressive. On the 26th they had lunch at the Star and Garter in Richmond, overlooking the Thames, and took a drive to Hampton Court. On the 27th, watching a cricket match at Lord's, Arthur was interrupted by the arrival of a telegram announcing the death of the Island's Governor. He must have wondered if Lord Henniker had carried out the instructions of the Keys to recommend him for 'Coronation Honours'. Presumably, but his name was not on the list of new knighthoods which appeared on the 26th. Arthur claimed in his diary that he was not surprised. In any case, he and Louisa had to travel back to the Isle of Man to attend Lord Henniker's funeral on 29 June.

The coronation was re-scheduled for 9 August after the king's recovery.

Three days before, Arthur had still not received his ticket for a seat in the abbey, so he wrote to the Earl Marshal, the Duke of Norfolk, who was in charge of arrangements, and heard by telegram that his ticket had gone to his London hotel. He travelled overnight to arrive in time, and having collected his ticket had breakfast with two of Louisa's siblings, Helena Ring and Cyril Hughes-Games, before claiming his seat in the north gallery of the nave. He could not see the actual ceremony, but could see most of the distinguished people present as they entered and left the abbey. This was another magnificent and colourful spectacle, especially as everyone present had to be in uniform or court dress, with no dark suits. The congregation 'made a perfect blaze of colour, chiefly scarlet and white'.

He recorded, 'The King looked pale, but walked, or rather rolled, along in great style. The Queen was as youthful and beautiful as ever, but how much is due to art and how much to nature I cannot say! ... The Princess of Wales [the future Queen Mary] is a much better-looking woman than I had supposed from her portraits. The Prince [the future George V] is an insignificant little chap who looks considerably shorter than his wife'. Moore's reverence for the institution of monarchy clearly did not inhibit him from recording irreverent personal comments in his diary.

The coronation might well have been the high point of Arthur Moore's year, had it not been for the extraordinary and entirely unexpected events which occurred just over a fortnight later, and which he recounted at very great length.[3] On Thursday 24 August, 'On returning home a little after 5 p.m. with Louisa I caught sight of the royal standard on a yacht entering the bay [which at that time would have been in full view from Woodbourne House]. I knew at once that the King must be on board and so I hurried down to the shore and went off on a small [boat]'. He arrived at the royal yacht, the *Victoria & Albert*, to find it 'surrounded by a yelling crowd of trippers' and about to sail off. Moore made himself known and asked if he could be of service to the king. This was not, perhaps, unduly presumptuous as the Island was without a Governor and the Acting Governor, Sir James Gell, was seventy-six and lived in Castletown. The royal equerry said the king would like to go for a drive on the Island from Ramsey the next day. After five minutes Moore was summoned to meet the king, who shook hands and introduced him to the queen and to Austen Chamberlain, MP, President of the Board of Trade, apparently the Cabinet member-in-waiting. They agreed a provisional route for the drive, the king asked Moore to act as his guide, and 'I told him that the yelling crowd which surrounded the yacht were trippers and not Manx people'. Moore left the royal yacht, arranged for two carriages and their drivers from Cronkbourne and

Woodbourne House to be taken to Ramsey for the use of the royal party, had a meeting with the Island's police chief, and sent a message to Sir James Gell to acquaint him with the arrangements.

The next morning Louisa, Edith, Rosie, Mildred and Arthur all caught the 8am train to Ramsey, where they met Sir James. Moore and Gell went onto the Queen's Pier, met the equerry, Captain Seymour Fortescue, and finally agreed on a drive to Peel via Bishopscourt, an open-air lunch at Peel Castle, on to Douglas, and back to Ramsey by electric train. 'But', said the equerry, 'the King and Queen are very keen on their tea. Where can they get tea near Douglas?' Quick as a flash, Moore suggested 'Cronkbourne!' His instinctive response was to propose his mother's house, the family seat, rather than his own home. He and Sir James looked round the yacht 'which is most luxuriously furnished. The cabins are fitted up with white satin'. They met some of the officers, the Marquis de Soveral, the Portuguese Ambassador and an intimate of the king's, and the Hon. Mrs Derek Keppel, 'a charming pretty little woman' who was reading an account of the Isle of Man in the *Encyclopaedia Britannica*. This was the king's favourite mistress, better known today as Alice Keppel, accompanied by her presumably long-suffering husband, the Hon. Major Derek Keppel. If Arthur Moore was aware of this arrangement, he gave no hint of it in his diary.

At 11am the king, the queen and their eldest daughter Princess Victoria, with the rest of their entourage, came ashore. Louisa Moore presented the queen with a bouquet. The party got into four carriages, the first two of which had to be dragged down the Queen's Pier by men because the horses refused to set foot on it. The Bishop and the Chief Constable followed in a fifth carriage, 'and Mr Hall Caine followed in a hired trap. I should mention that Mr Hall Caine attached himself (uninvited) to the party'. At this point in his narrative Moore digressed, barely able to control his rage. Hall Caine had written to the king offering to act as his guide, and had been invited to attend the lunch at Peel Castle. 'H.C. took advantage of this to join the party, to place himself in the group [photograph] that was taken at Bishops-court, to, as far as he could, monopolise the King and Queen at Peel Castle, and to influence all the English newspapers to represent him as their Majesties' guide, philosopher and friend throughout! From the point of view of his public he has no doubt scored'. Moore was friendly with Hall Caine before and after this event, but he was very annoyed that the novelist was encroaching on what he considered his own official role.

The party stopped for half an hour at Bishopscourt where, in addition to having a group photograph taken by the Ramsey photographer G. B. Cowen, the king and queen and some of their courtiers ate sandwiches. The carriages moved on and eventually arrived at Peel harbour, then drove round to the castle where lunch was served at about 2.45pm on the slope to the south of the ruined cathedral. One imagines the servants unloading and opening well-stocked hampers of food and drink, and perhaps deck chairs. Moore continues: 'The King signed to me to come and sit on his right hand and he certainly proved a most genial and delightful host, pressing his guests to help themselves and entertaining them by his conversation'. Moore recorded virtually every word the king said to him; questions about the Island, remarks about the Archbishop of Canterbury, the English in Egypt, Dean Stanley in Palestine, English and French national characters. 'After the meal excellent coffee was provided, made by an Egyptian wearing a fez, cigars and cigarettes were offered, whisky-and-sodas were drunk, and port was handed round'.

Captain Fortescue approached the king and said, 'I fear, Sir, it is getting too late to go round by Douglas'. Moore: 'But Sir, you have promised to honour me'. 'The King put his hand on my arm and said "I am coming to you, and will drive through part of Douglas"'. On the road from Peel to the Quarterbridge the party were annoyed by a crowd of cyclists who kicked up a tremendous dust. At Cronkbourne Moore introduced the king and queen to his family, and 'took the king to the lavatory downstairs, knowing that he would prefer not to go upstairs. It was horribly dark and he stumbled about, but was most absolutely kind and good natured'. The king said Cronkbourne was a very pretty place, and the queen told Moore he had a very pretty wife. At some later date, the royal visit was commemorated by an inscription over the fireplace in the hall.

Amid scenes of great enthusiasm, the royal party drove through Douglas to the tramway station at Derby Castle at about 6.30pm. 'Sir James Gell and I went into the car to say goodbye when it went off with a sudden jerk and I was thrown right across the King's knees'. The Marquis de Soveral pulled Moore to his feet, shouting 'I save your life, I save your life!' Everyone, king and queen included, burst out laughing. The car stopped further on, where Sir James and Arthur Moore had 'a most cordial farewell from the King and Queen'. Moore gave the king his *A History of the Isle of Man*, and the queen *The Story of the Isle of Man* – the version intended for schoolchildren.

Some days later Moore received several elaborately courtly thank-you letters. 'The Queen has been very busy reading your invaluable book'. Alice Keppel hoped to return to the Island. Austen Chamberlain agreed that it was a pity each had not known the other was an Old Rugbeian.

On 18 September news arrived that 'His Majesty has conferred the honour of a Commandership of the Royal Victorian Order upon me. It or

One of the most exciting days of A. W. Moore's life came when King Edward VII and Queen Alexandra, sailing past the Island on the royal yacht *Victoria & Albert* on 24 August 1902, decided to pay an unofficial visit. The yacht was first sighted in Douglas Bay, and in the Governor's absence from the Island Arthur Moore, as Speaker, went on board to greet the king and queen and the next day rushed to Ramsey to welcome them again when they disembarked. He spent the entire day with the royal couple (taking a dim view of attempts by Hall Caine, with his son in the centre of this photograph, to muscle in on the occasion), and even brought them home for tea with his mother at Cronkbourne

in the afternoon. The royal party included, as one of the king's equerries, the Hon. Major Derek Keppel (far right, next to A. W. Moore), but the great and good of the Isle of Man may not have been entirely aware of the role played by his wife, the Hon. Alice Keppel (far left, next to Princess Victoria). She had been the king's favourite mistress since 1898. The Right Hon. Austen Chamberlain, elder brother of Neville Chamberlain (at the far back, behind Hall Caine), was also one of the party, as was the colourful Marquis de Soveral (in bowler hat, behind the king), the Portuguese ambassador and confidant of both King Edward and Queen Alexandra.

Arthur's sister Rosie and wife Louisa curtseying at the front door of Cronkbourne as the king doffs his hat and is driven away. Queen Alexandra, Princess Victoria and the Marquis de Soveral are also in the carriage, having taken tea with Hannah Moore and her family at the end of a strenuous day's sightseeing.

any other honour was completely unexpected. It gives me rank above the Companions of the Bath and next below Knight Bachelor. To my mind it is a much higher honour than a knighthood'. He did not mention, then or later, that the same honour was also bestowed upon Sir James Gell. In November he received by post the formal warrant of the CVO, signed by the king, together with the statutes of the order. On 18 May 1903 he went to a levée at Buckingham Palace to receive the CVO insignia. He wrote hopefully, 'I rather think from his expression that the King recognised me, but I cannot feel sure'. He took pleasure in wearing his decoration on official occasions for the rest of his life.

Arthur Moore was definitely a 'Somebody', but the solemnity and usually unconscious humour of his diary, and the very human vanity and vulnerability it displays, can sometimes recall a better-known diarist, his fictional contemporary Charles Pooter.[4]

The fashionable London society artist Charles Goldsborough Anderson was commissioned to produce portraits of Arthur and Louisa in 1902 and 1903. Arthur considered that his own, produced in only two sittings, was a good likeness ('He paints marvellously quickly'), but his comment on Louisa's was, 'It is a success *on the whole*, though there is a reddish tinge in the hair which does not exist, the nose is not right, and the expression missed'.

Chapter 9

LAST YEARS

The years from 1902 to 1909, which turned out to be the last seven years of Arthur Moore's life, were also the years in which the 'Manx struggle for reform' began in earnest.[1] For several years there had been signs of public opinion moving in favour of change in the Island's political system. The appointment as Governor of Lord Raglan, an old-school Tory diehard opposed to virtually all measures of political and social reform, brought into being the Manx National Reform League, led by Samuel Norris.[2] Manx politics became more polarised than ever before, and Arthur Moore, as Speaker of the House of Keys, was at the eye of the storm.

Initially Lord Raglan made a good impression on Moore, who met him when he disembarked in Douglas on 8 September 1902, for his first, preliminary, unofficial visit to the Island. The next day he came to lunch at Cronkbourne, and drove over with the Moores to Bishopscourt, to spend two nights there with other Island dignitaries. Moore found him 'a most pleasant and entertaining man – great on sport and on military matters'.

Raglan's personal charm and affability were his outstanding asset throughout his time as Governor. On 21 October he was back in the Island, this time with Lady Raglan, for his official installation by Sir James Gell, Acting Governor, at the Court House in Castle Rushen. Sir James now became his deputy, and hosted a lunch, 'in fact a very lengthy dinner', for thirty-five people, including Arthur and Louisa Moore, at his house on the Parade in Castletown. About a month later, however, Lord Raglan, aged forty-five, became seriously ill and had to return to London for medical treatment.[3] Gell was again appointed Acting Governor, and was in charge of the Island's affairs for seven months until June 1903.

During the winter of 1903 Arthur Moore continued to carry out his duties as Speaker, presiding over the passage through the Keys in January of the new Election Act, which increased the Island's electorate to 46% of the adult population, and reduced the period between elections from seven to five years. As Samuel Norris wrote, 'In winding up the session in April 1903 the Speaker congratulated the House on setting a record by passing nine Acts – the most important being the enactment of household suffrage for Keys elections'; in future there would be at least one vote per household, though not yet one person, one vote.[4]

In mid-May Arthur and Louisa Moore left the Island for a month's holiday. They spent a weekend near Lichfield with Arthur's sister Dolly and her husband Bassett Seckham, moving on to London where Arthur received his CVO from the king at Buckingham Palace. They then headed for Paris, and thence to Switzerland where they spent between two and three weeks touring, by rail and lake steamers. They arrived back in London on 8 June and stayed for the next week at the Langham Hotel in Portland Place. This was not for the usual family visits, theatres and art galleries. 'My time was chiefly spent in going to and from Dr. Symonds who operated on me twice for polypi in the nose – painful and trying, but successful – and in interviewing the London agents'. Charles Symonds was a pioneering surgeon at Guy's Hospital who showed amazing skill in removing nasal polyps and largyngeal tumours.[5] Moore had found the best man in the medical profession for his particular ailment, but the problem was to recur with increasing severity. For the rest of his life, he was battling against ill health. Meanwhile, Louisa sat for a portrait by Charles Goldsborough Anderson, the artist who had painted Arthur's portrait the previous year.

They arrived home on 16 June, nine days after the return of Lord Raglan. There had been important political developments during their absence. When the financial statement was discussed in Tynwald on 29 May, Sir James Gell, presiding over the proceedings, sprang a surprise on members by claiming there was a need for more revenue. The First Deemster, Thomas Kneen, proposed the imposition of a sugar tax (then being paid in England on account of the Boer War) to bring in an extra £10,400 a year, about a fifteen per cent increase in the Island's total national taxation.

There were strong protests from some members of the Keys. As William Goldsmith pointed out, 'there was no sugar tax imposed in England until there were death duties and income tax... It is not fair to bring in a tax like this, which affects the working classes and the people of the Island, until there is some tax on people who have money'. He also said that the tax was unnecessary, since only £1,500 extra revenue was needed, not £10,500. Other members complained about the number of well-paid, unelected, officials and civil servants who sat on the Legislative Council. Sir James Gell was eighty years old, but still a determined and clever political operator. He kept the Keys in session till late in the evening, and re-convened Tynwald the next day, having summoned absentees to attend.

Arthur and Louisa Moore in an uncomfortably-posed group picture taken in early September 1902, when Lord Raglan, as Governor-elect, paid an unofficial visit to the Island. He came to lunch at Cronkbourne, and the Moores later drove him over to Bishopscourt where they stayed for two nights; Moore would later become one of Raglan's most vigorous opponents, but they remained socially cordial. Lord Raglan is the tall figure in the back row. Louisa sits in front of Arthur in the front row (right) between Sir James Gell, Attorney-General, and Colonel Anderson. Lord Raglan was officially installed as Governor by Sir James at Castle Rushen on 21 October.

Eventually the Keys were bullied into recording the necessary minimum of thirteen votes for the sugar tax. This provoked them to pass for the first time a motion calling for reform of the Legislative Council. They demanded that the Vicar General and the Archdeacon should no longer be members ex officio, that they should be replaced by members nominated by the Keys, and that the Vicar-General's salary should not be paid from government funds. Both of these were Anglican appointments. The Keys, having passed the motion by twelve votes to seven, forwarded it to the Home Secretary with the request that the Crown should approve of the Keys initiating legislation along these lines. Six weeks later the Home Secretary told the Governor that he would not intervene. His letter was passed on to the House of Keys.[6]

It is overwhelmingly probable that Sir James Gell consulted the absent Lord Raglan before introducing the sugar tax proposal. It is also quite likely that he chose to do so at a time when Arthur Moore, the elected Speaker of the Keys and their defender against encroachments by the Council or the Governor, was absent from the Island.

Moore, true to form, did not record his thoughts on these developments in his diary when he returned to the Island. But, quite apart from the merits of the issues, the situation must have been fraught with family embarrassment for him. Louisa's elder sister Helena was married to George Ring, who had become Attorney-General, and as such a member of the Legislative Council, in 1898, and who was one of the Governor's most determined and articulate advisers. The position of Vicar-General, a paid sinecure, was held by the eighty-eight year old Samuel Harris, High Bailiff of Douglas. His heir apparent, who at about this time was given a post in the Vicar-General's office, was Louisa's younger brother Cyril Hughes-Games – thought to have been promoted through the influence of George Ring. Harris eventually died in office in 1905, at the age of ninety, and Cyril Hughes-Games became Vicar-General in 1906 at the age of thirty-six.

Members of the Council may have hoped that Arthur Moore's family connections would serve to moderate his defence of the rights of the House of Keys, but if so they had mistaken their man. His diary entry on Tynwald Day was bland and conventional: 'This was Lord Raglan's first appearance in public as governor. He conducted the business of this Court, and of those on the 14th and 15th, very well'. Ever since he could remember, Moore must have been used to a regime in which the competence, views and personality of the Governor were the most important aspects of Manx politics. But what he did not mention in his diary entry was that he interrupted Bishop Straton's reply to a question on the Vicar-General issue when the Bishop began to attack by name the MHK J. D. Clucas, who had moved the reform motion, and who had no right to reply to the Bishop on that occasion.

The deliberations of the Keys for the rest of the session, that is for a week or so in July and a fortnight in September/October, were mainly concerned not with reform but with the extension of the boundaries of Douglas, the purchase and alteration of Government House, and yet another licensing bill. Moore was away a good deal on a mixture of business and pleasure. He regretfully declined a suggestion from Hall Caine that he should accompany the novelist on a trip to Iceland: 'It is a very great temptation, but I do not like to go away from home again after the, for me, long holiday in Switzerland'. But he went to Belfast in August on Steam Packet, and also factory, business, finding time for some golf and cycling, and also travelled over to Barrow for the launch of a ship.

In September he was away for ten days; first he visited Louisa's younger sister Winifred and her husband Stanley Appleby at Norton, near Stockton-on-Tees. They went for runs in Stanley's motor car and played golf. Arthur thought West Hartlepool, Middlesborough and Sunderland were 'all more or less ghastly places', and worse looked at from a business point of view; the shipping was largely 'tramps which use the vilest shoddy in the way of canvas'. After calling to see his sick father-in-law in Leeds, he joined other Steam Packet directors in London to see a new turbine boat at Dover, and slipped across the Channel for a couple of days in Calais, Boulogne and Dunkirk.

Meanwhile at home the pressure for reform was mounting. The socialist monthly journal, *The Manx Reformer*, claimed a circulation of 2,000 copies, mainly in Douglas. Samuel Norris's five articles on Manx Home Rule as it worked in practice, and the urgent need for reform, had appeared in the *Liverpool Weekly Mercury*, which at that time circulated widely in the Island, between 30 May and 28 June. In October, with the general election approaching, Norris issued the articles in a penny pamphlet, 'Manxland's Home Rule Parliament', adding to it a detailed reform programme. At the same time he took steps to set up the Manx National Reform League with himself as secretary; he organised public meetings and wrote to every election candidate to ascertain their views and solicit their support.[7]

The Keys were dissolved at the end of October. Yet again, there was no contested election in Middle, but Dalrymple Maitland, reformer, William Hutchinson, more conservative, and Arthur Moore all responded to the Reform League's questions. Their replies have not survived, but one account of the reform movement claims that Moore 'remained non-committal about the League and its programme of reform'.[8] Moore, as Speaker in the old parliament and unanimously re-elected in the new one, would not have thought it appropriate to align himself wholly with any outside pressure group, even had he agreed with all their proposals. His views on current politics were stated at the usual public meetings held by the candidates at Onchan, Braddan and Santon. He reviewed the previous seven years, and said the Factory Act had not yet been passed because it was such a huge piece of legislation, more appropriate to England; what the Island needed, in his view, was a simple Workshops Act, to regulate the hours of labour, protect workmen from machinery, and provide for adequate sanitation. On Employers' Liability, he agreed that Manx labourers needed the same protection as their English counterparts (applause). The Island was short of money because there was no direct taxation; he supported the introduction of death duties. He would back any reasonable scheme for introducing a representative element into the Legislative Council. He and his colleagues were all in favour of retaining the common lands, keeping rivers clear to avoid flooding, and introducing a small tax on bicycles.[9]

These views established Moore as being broadly on the progressive side of the argument, as were a clear majority of the new House of Keys which assembled in December. It was now up to the members to respond to the public pressure for reform. On 1 March 1904 a committee of seven MHKs, including Hall Caine and Tom Cormode, was set up to report and make recommendations on legislative and administrative reform, with a view to extending popular control. Their interim report in July recommended that there was no need for four different High Bailiffs on the Island – one stipendiary magistrate would do. Their much fuller report in December recommended, among other things, the appointment of Governors for a fixed term only, an end to the Governor's sole control of the police, the abolition of one of the two Deemsters, and a Legislative Council with an elected majority.

Meanwhile Arthur Moore made a proposal in July for a committee of enquiry into taxation policy, which was carried through the Keys by twenty votes to one. It was carried through the Council only by the casting vote of the Governor, who made it plain, however, that whatever the committee suggested, he would remain ultimately responsible. Moore, who was himself appointed to the committee, declared that the existing method of raising revenue was insecure and unjust to the poor. 'I have not rushed at this matter. I have brought it forward with considerable diffidence and reluctance ... and I have only done so at last from an overwhelming sense of public duty'.[10]

The slow progress of these committee deliberations on reform left time for private life. The year started badly, for Louisa especially, with the death of her brother Joshua at Cheltenham in early January, followed by the death of her father, Joshua the elder, in Hull at the end of March. She and Arthur attended both funerals, and her widowed mother came back to the Island to live at Homefield in Douglas.

A cheerful diversion was provided by motor races held in May; Arthur, Louisa and young Arthur watched the races, and were impressed by the cars coming down from 'Penny-Pot' (Beinn-y-Phott) at about 70mph. Later in the month, Arthur took his wife and son to Harrogate before heading for France to select a finishing school near Paris for Helen. He also enjoyed a week's holiday exploring Rheims, Troyes and Fontainebleau, where he spent three days, visiting the chateau and then hiring a bicycle and cycling, in all, about 100 miles in and around the Forêt de Fontainebleau. For the first time, he made a collection of picture postcards of his trip. After the Pan-Celtic Congress in Caernarvon (Chapter 7) he and Louisa took the boat from the Isle of Man to Barrow, and spent a weekend with the Lewthwaites, friends of Arthur's, at Broughton-in-Furness.

He also found time for some 'literary work' in 1904, producing two minor publications. His *Historical Account of the Isle of Man Steam Packet Company Limited 1830-1904* is a succinct account, commissioned by his fellow directors and profusely illustrated with pictures of ships and their officers. *Douglas 100 Years Ago*, reprinted from articles in the *Manx Sun*, is a thirty-five page miscellany edited by Moore to give 'An Account Illustrative of Manx Life and Manners at that Period Compiled from Various Authorities both Printed and Manuscript'.

By the end of the year Helen was installed at her Paris finishing school, Margery had followed in her footsteps to Cheltenham Ladies College, and little Arthur was still at home, at nine the apple of his father's eye. In mid-March, the diarist records, 'Arthur has been in bed since the beginning of the month with a chill to the kidneys. It is a case of care and keeping warm'. In early August, 'I took little Arthur for a trip round the Island [presumably by boat] which he greatly enjoyed', and on 15 September, 'Arthur put on boy's clothes for the first time'. Christmas was spent at Cronkbourne with 'the usual schoolchildren's entertainment' on Christmas Eve. A querulous note, possibly reflecting his worsening health, is sounded by Moore's final comment for 1904: 'The carol nuisance has been worse than ever this year. It went on for a full fortnight before Christmas and the singing gets steadily worse'.

In 1905 it began to look as though there might soon be some progress on the issue of constitutional reform. The Keys debated the report of the Reform Committee on 21 March, beginning with the machinery of justice: the Speaker wanted to keep both Deemsters and instead abolish the High Bailiffs, but he was outvoted. The House voted to have a single stipendiary magistrate for the whole Island, to reduce the number of Deemsters from two to one, to prohibit the Attorney-General from private practice, and to require him to be available to advise both branches of Tynwald and its Boards. They also wanted an English barrister of standing to serve on the Court of Appeal, instead of the judge whose decision was the subject of appeal.

Moore advised the House, perhaps unwisely, that this was enough to be going on with, and that rather than present their whole reform programme, they should first petition the Home Secretary on these proposals alone. This was done, and in July it was announced that the Home Secretary had agreed to meet a deputation from the Keys to discuss their petition. On 19 July Arthur Moore travelled down to London as chairman of the deputation, which also included Hall Caine and William Goldsmith, in order to meet the Conservative Home Secretary, Aretas Akers-Douglas. The meeting took place at the Home Office at noon, with Akers-Douglas and several junior ministers and officials. 'There was nothing formal about the meeting and everyone was most friendly and courteous. I gave the views of the Keys at some length, my colleagues added a few words, and we replied to questions'. Arthur Moore then had lunch with Hall Caine at his club in Whitehall, went to Lords to see part of the Lancashire v. Middlesex county cricket match, and returned to the home of his hosts, Frank and Cissie Pearson. Was he perhaps lulled by his friendly reception into unwarranted optimism? In a letter dated 12 September, which reached the Keys via the Governor on 9 October, Akers-Douglas refused the deputation's requests, agreeing only to consider the function of the Attorney-General next time there was a vacancy. A Conservative Home Secretary would not act against the wishes of a Conservative colonial governor.

There was, perhaps, greater reason for rational hope when the Tynwald Taxation Committee, set up at Moore's suggestion in July 1904, reported back in October 1905. The committee, chaired by George Ring, recognised that indirect taxation on tea, sugar and tobacco bore heavily on the lower classes, and recommended the introduction of estate duty, income tax, and a general tax on real estate. The report now awaited discussion by both the Council and the Keys.

Other aspects of Moore's life must have given him more enjoyment than the long-drawn-out struggle for reform. When he went over to Liverpool for

Steam Packet Company meetings, he was usually able to enjoy some golf and to stay either at the Palace Hotel, Birkdale, or The Gables, Fulwood Park, the home of an old Trinity friend, W. S. Patterson, and his wife. Patterson was a corn merchant and one-time Lancashire county cricketer. In May Moore enjoyed the Isle of Man motor races again. The emphasis was on cars: on 31 May he noted that 'The motor bicycle races held in the early morning were a fiasco, none of the cycles being able to complete the entire route'. His own unmotorised cycling continued to be successful. After a visit to Newcastle-upon-Tyne for trials of the SS *Viking*, built by Armstrong Whitworth, he hastened south in mid-June to catch some Australian cricket in London. He then cycled in the Thames Valley for five days, from Maidenhead to Oxford and Cirencester, hill-climbing over the chalk downs between Swindon and Hungerford, returning through Boxhill and back to London for a rendezvous with Louisa and five nights at the Great Central Hotel. He thought the churches in Surrey were not equal to those in Oxfordshire or Gloucestershire, but 'all this country [was] lovely'. He averaged about sixty miles a day on his bicycle. When he and Louisa crossed back to the Island on the 26th it was on the maiden voyage of the *Viking*, only twelve days after she completed her trials on the Tyne. And he fitted in a week in Scotland in September, including Iona and Staffa, a railway trip from Fort William back to Oban, Skye, Inverness and Pitlochry, Perth and Arbroath, and across the Tay Bridge to St Andrews. Moore must have plotted his holiday itineraries meticulously, by rail and by boat.

In October he dined or lunched with Lord Raglan on several occasions, whether as the result of a charm offensive by the Governor or the cementing of a strictly non-political friendship. On the 11th he showed Raglan round the Tromode works. New responsibilities began on 13 October, when he was unanimously elected Chairman of the Hospital Committee. 'I have accepted the post very unwillingly, but, in view of the very important negotiations with Noble's Trustees with regard to the building of a new hospital, I suppose it is my duty to do so'. He was also involved with Noble's will as one of the three Trustees who had £10,000 left to them for the purpose of building a new church in Douglas. This was to be St Ninian's, the architect being Moore's friend W. D. Caröe. The only publication he found time to see through the press in 1905 was *Notes and Documents from the Records of the Isle of Man*, a compilation of odds and ends left over from his research which appeared in the *Manx Sun*, and was published by that newspaper in booklet form before it ceased publication.

The children continued to be a source of pride and sometimes of apprehension. Helen arrived home from Paris in July, and Arthur went to

Liverpool to meet her. 'She looks very well and is much improved in manner and appearance. She has done remarkably well at school, having got five first prizes'. Helen was now seventeen. Margery, still at Cheltenham and sixteen in September, seems to have occasioned least comment. At the end of the summer term she had a cough and was not looking well; by Christmas she was looking very well, but still had the remains of whooping cough. In July Arthur Moore combined a stay with John Rhys and his wife Elspeth at Jesus College, Oxford, with an inspection of Mr Lynam's Preparatory School, nowadays better known as the Dragon School. He decided that Mr Lynam was 'a pleasant, capable man' and that his charges 'seemed to be nice gentlemanly boys', though he was 'not very much taken' with Mrs Sharp, Arthur's prospective landlady, who appeared unsympathetic. However, Arthur was to share his lodgings with two cousins, the sons of Revd Stephen Hughes-Games, so Louisa took him to school in Oxford in September, and was going to stay with him until he was 'quite settled'. 'I shall miss him terribly', wrote his father. In November both parents were alarmed because young Arthur had a severe cold, and in early December Louisa went to Oxford again to fetch him home early, though it turned out there was very little the matter with him. There may have been too much fussing over Arthur, but perhaps he was a delicate boy, as his father had been. The Moores had already lost one son, and Arthur was only ten.

The year 1905 ended with the same complaints about carol singing, and also with a declaration of Moore's literary tastes, not in the diary but in Quine's notes, and reproduced in his preface to *Nessy Heywood*. There seems to have been some sort of ongoing collaboration between Moore and Quine, who was allowed to read Moore's diaries, perhaps annually, and to ask questions about them. The arrangement may have started after Moore became Speaker. Presumably there was an understanding that Quine might write a biographical sketch, as he did; thus Moore's diary may be less artless than it appears. Looking through the diary, apparently at the end of 1905, he realised there were no notes on reading, 'my greatest hobby'. So he seems virtually to have dictated a statement to Quine (Appendix IV, page 163).

The election of a reforming Liberal government in Britain at the beginning of 1906 put new heart into the Keys. But the first controversial issue of the year was the Island's education policy. Arthur Moore took education very seriously, and wanted to see effective progress, especially in secondary education, under the direction of a single Board of Education. He resigned from the Council of Education in January because the legislature did not support his policy, but was prevailed upon to accept re-election by Tynwald, which was unanimous.

In February the Keys considered the report of the Taxation Committee. They supported its recommendations in principle *nem. con.*, but did not pass an amendment asking the Governor to introduce a bill. This inconsistency annoyed Arthur Moore, who remarked in his diary that there was not much point in the House being in favour of death duties in principle if they were not prepared to support them 'in the concrete or actual form'. Even in a reforming House of Keys, the habit of deference to the Governor was deeply rooted. At the end of May the Governor presented his annual financial statement: he proposed to reduce the duty on tea, put additional duties on tobacco and spirits, and leave the sugar tax unchanged. He had no intention of making any further changes for the time being, did not accept the report of the Taxation Committee, and was unmoved by Moore's speech in Tynwald in favour of productive expenditure, education and training for the young, and proper development of the Island's resources.

Meanwhile, at the end of February the new Liberal Home Secretary Herbert Gladstone wrote to the Keys concerning their requests of 1905 for reforming the judiciary. He could not agree to piecemeal changes, he said, and would only consider such issues as the position of the Vicar-General as part of a scheme for the general revision of the Island's constitution. Arthur Moore reiterated his position in a memorandum concerning the Vicar-General and the Archdeacon which he read to the Keys. In this he deployed historical evidence, pointing out that the Vicar-General had only been paid from Government funds since 1846. But in view of Herbert Gladstone's letter, reformers' hopes had now veered back towards full-blown constitutional reform. On 27 March the Keys came out with all guns blazing: they wanted the Governor appointed for a fixed term of years, and a new scheme of taxation and expenditure, with a new Executive Council drawn from both Houses to advise the Governor and moderate what Moore described as his 'almost autocratic' authority. Moore himself would have been content with a representative element on the Council to start with, but the majority in the Keys wanted the majority of the Council to be elected. A Police Board should be set up, they demanded, and civil servants' salaries should not be altered without the consent of Tynwald. A committee of five, which included the Speaker, was deputed to approach the Governor before these demands were sent to London.

But Arthur Moore was very tired. 'Not having been well for some time past I was recommended by Dr Hamilton to go to the south of France for a time'. His fortnight's holiday in April was probably more energetic than his doctor had in mind. He took a train from Paris to Toulouse and moved on to the ancient walled city of Carcassonne, where he read a pamphlet on the restoration of the fortifications by Viollet-le-Duc which Lord Raglan had lent him. He spent six days in Montpellier, remarking that he was 'never in a town with more hairdressers and fewer blacksmiths', and used it as a centre for excursions to the mediaeval port of Aigues-Mortes and the Roman amphitheatres at Arles and Nîmes. He returned north via Clermont-Ferrand, Nevers and Bourges, collecting Helen from her school and visiting more churches, a museum and the opera in Paris. He fitted in the quarterly Steam Packet meeting in Liverpool before returning home on 21 April.

Moore certainly needed reserves of strength to draw upon on his return. On 10 May 'A meeting between the Governor and myself with a Committee of the House of Keys to discuss the resolutions on Constitutional Reform proved quite futile, the Governor being against us on practically every point'. The only point Raglan would accept was that the Attorney-General should in future give advice to Boards set up by Tynwald. The Legislative Council refused the Keys' request for an informal joint conference and replied that they could debate the issues in Tynwald. At the end of May the Keys agreed to set up another committee which would prepare a comprehensive petition to the Home Secretary. Moore, arguing from historical precedent once more, maintained that the House of Keys had the right to approach the Crown, the Home Office, the Treasury or Parliament whenever it wished, without the Governor's permission. Tempers were getting very heated, and although Moore was initially against it, the Keys agreed to adjourn for four weeks before resuming their discussions.

Arthur Moore was not a natural rebel, and it gave him no pleasure to find himself confronting the Governor in an antagonistic way. At the same time he was facing another difficult moment of decision. The firm of W. F. Moore and Son was still advertising itself confidently as the Island's leading private company in the publication *Mercantile Manxland* (1900). But in the new century the family business was causing him increasing anxiety. By August 1903, when he visited a number of different factories in Belfast, he was clearly keen to save money. In November that year he travelled to London to introduce his new agents to various customers. But at last, in May 1906, he had to accept the inevitable, that the firm was losing money and was no longer viable. One reason for this was the cost of importing flax, the raw material of sailcloth; the main producers were no longer in Ireland, but in Holland, Belgium and Russia. There had at one time been 120 workers at Tromode; now there were only eighty. On 5 May they all received notice that the mills would close down on 30 June. Taking into account their families, about 250 people, almost all living in Cronkbourne Village, were affected.

Arthur Moore did what he could to soften the blow by offering modest pensions, to be assessed on a case-by-case basis, to those employed for over twenty years and unable to rely on support from their families. For those who had served for more than thirty years, widows and the long-term sick, rent-free tenure for life of the Cronkbourne cottages was also offered. Those who wished to seek work outside the Island were offered free passage to Liverpool, Glasgow or Belfast. There were, of course, still no old age pensions in the Island, which remained one of the labour movement's unfulfilled demands. The *Examiner* headed its report, 'Tromode Mills to Be Closed – A Generous Employer – Parting a Terrible Wrench'.[11] Moore must have found it so, with his strong sense of family, knowing that he was closing down the firm which had sustained his own family for 116 years. For the time being, though, 'it is a great relief to me, but I am very sorry for the workpeople ... it will be very difficult to get work for many of them'. He sold the goodwill of the firm to a sailcloth works based in Somerset.

Possibly he was happy to be out of the Island as much as possible in June, when the last few weeks of W. F. Moore and Son coincided with the four weeks' recess of the Keys. He and Louisa went to London for a few days, then to Oxford where young Arthur, who had already been visited in March because he had chickenpox, now had an attack of German measles. From Oxford Arthur travelled by train to Worcester before starting a week's cycle tour in the Welsh Borders via Malvern, Brecon, the upper Wye Valley, Radnorshire, Ludlow, Bridgnorth, Shrewsbury, Llangollen and Chester. Presumably this helped take his mind off his problems.

Moore presided over a Keys debate on 26 June which voted that the seven-strong petition committee (including Hall Caine, Tom Cormode and William Goldsmith) should prepare a petition to the Home Secretary for constitutional reform; the motion was carried by fifteen votes to five, Moore himself being one of the five who would have preferred further discussion in Tynwald before taking this action. But he had scarcely been in the Island for a week before he had to hurry back to London for a few days, missing Tynwald Day, for the funeral of Henry Christian; his seventy-four year old uncle had died suddenly after suffering three strokes in rapid succession. Back in the Island, on 10 July, he was visited by Sir William Agnew and went on board his fine 300-ton steam yacht, the *Greta*.

A few days later, on 13 July, 'I underwent an operation for the removal of a tumour in my mouth and polypi in my nose. I was under ether for an hour, the operator being Dr Sharp from Leeds, a specialist in such matters. I felt distinctly shaky for some days afterwards'. He convalesced by staying for a few days with Frank and Cissie Pearson in their country cottage near

Pangbourne in the Thames Valley, then collected young Arthur from Oxford on his way home. Margery had left Cheltenham, and Helen also arrived home on the Island, having now left school for good.

It may have been during August, when nothing is recorded in his diary, that Moore produced the last publication drawn from his contributions to the *Manx Sun*. *The Letters of Bishop Hildesley 1755-1772* consisted of eighty-six previously unpublished letters from the Bishop to Revd Philip Moore, an ancestor of Arthur's, which were in his personal collection. This foolscap booklet of 110 pages is said to have been printed in an edition of only twenty-five copies. No doubt, as with most of his books, Moore paid the costs of printing and publication of this work of very limited circulation.

In early September he was off again for a week's cycling in southern Scotland, including Dumfries, Peebles, and Sir Walter Scott's home at Abbotsford, where he complained that he had had to go round the house with a group of Germans who 'quacked' loudly. Later in the month young Arthur started as a boarder at King William's College, where he seemed to settle down much more happily than he did at Oxford, and Louisa took Margery to London on her way to her new school in Paris.

In October Hannah Moore, now eighty-two, suffered a stroke which paralysed her left side, but she was out of bed again within a fortnight, apparently indestructible. This was the last crisis of 1906. Young Arthur was enjoying himself at King William's, suffering nothing worse than a bad attack of indigestion from over-eating. There were no more crucial confrontations in Tynwald or the House of Keys before Christmas. Arthur Moore, with his sister-in-law Helena Ring, attended an entertainment held at Castle Rushen in October in honour of Lord Raglan's installation as Governor four years previously. A picnic lunch was held in the Council Chamber and lectures were given by Armitage Rigby, the architect who was restoring the castle, on its mediaeval fortifications, and by P. M. C. Kermode on runic crosses.[12] Such antiquarian interests were what Lord Raglan and Arthur Moore had in common. But although 1906 ended in a relatively conciliatory and peaceful fashion, it had been a very stressful year, and the issue of constitutional reform remained unresolved.

The year 1907 was in general a quieter one than its predecessor for Arthur Moore, and many of his diary entries describe uncontroversial ceremonial occasions of the kind he enjoyed, but the continuing deterioration of his health meant that he found life an increasingly uphill struggle. Despite occasional vigorous bouts of cycling he looked, in his fifties, to judge from surviving photographs, like an old man.

In January he spoke to the Liverpool Manx in favour of raising money for a memorial to T. E. Brown and, on Steam Packet business as usual, stayed for two days at the Vegetarian Home at Southport, where he was very comfortable and found the food good. Since Moore was not usually a vegetarian, the brief stay sounds rather like a rest cure for an invalid. In February young Arthur had bronchitis; the Earl of Lytton came to dinner before addressing a meeting in the Gaiety Theatre, chaired by Arthur senior, on 'Nationalisation of Public Houses', and at the end of the month Arthur and Louisa were asked, as the only guests, to Government House to celebrate Lord and Lady Raglan's wedding anniversary.

In March Moore addressed Tynwald for nearly an hour on the subject of harbour works in Douglas. He was strongly in favour of such development and of encouraging more visitors to the Island. He also spoke at a meeting held to promote Sunday observance, and again annoyed the extreme Sabbatarians by his liberal views. Helen sang in a duet at the Guild, but was too nervous to do justice to herself; she and her partner came third. The Raglans, the Moores, the Bishop and Mrs Straton combined to give a supper at the Castle Mona to about forty of the people chiefly connected with the Guild. At the end of March, Arthur crossed to Liverpool with the intention of attending the funeral of an ancient aunt living on the Wirral. In the event he missed it, but enjoyed a day's cycling on Good Friday to Hawarden, where he visited St Deiniol's Library, W. E. Gladstone's bequest to the nation. Politically, the most important development in March was the despatch of the Keys' reform petition, via the Governor, to the Home Office; they replied that it was receiving their attention.[13]

In April and May Tynwald focused on a new Education Bill which made provision for the expansion of secondary education to be organised through four local boards. Moore supported the Bill, and organised a public meeting in Onchan to discuss it with his constituents; there was a unanimous vote in favour. It passed through the Keys by fifteen votes to six, and became law later in the year.

In June, although it was 'the coldest June on record', Arthur set off on a fortnight's energetic cycle tour around Dorset and Somerset, visiting many churches and other antiquities, including hill forts such as Maiden Castle, the Undercliff at Lyme Regis, and other attractions. He thought the people of Dorset the most courteous in England. He enjoyed a brief stay and a motor car excursion to several villages with Cecil Hayward, the man to whom he had sold the goodwill of W. F. Moore and Son. Just as he had at school, he was pushing his strength to the limit.

In July Moore made perhaps his most forceful Tynwald speech of the year, strongly supporting the appointment of a Medical Officer of Health for the whole Island. As a farmer he was well aware of the problems of tuberculosis in cattle, and there was a need to educate public opinion on this subject. There were other controversial debates in Tynwald and in the Keys, but for the most part Arthur Moore contented himself with doing his job as Speaker without intervening in debates.

In August he enjoyed a visit to the Island by the Royal Navy, meeting Lord Charles Beresford, Admiral of the Fleet, and looking over the flagship, HMS *King Edward VII*. He presided over a luncheon for 500 of the sailors and a few officers in a tent in the grounds of the Villa Marina, and presented the prizes at sports held for the sailors at Kirby. The Admiral entertained Moore, Lord Raglan and others to 'a very magnificent and pleasant lunch' on board the flagship, and in the afternoon there was a large garden party at Government House.

At the end of August Moore spent just over a week cycling in and around the Wye Valley. Lord Raglan met him with a car at Hereford station, and he was driven to Monmouth where he stayed in a hotel and 'messed with the Royal Monmouth Engineers at the Castle'. This was presumably through Lord Raglan putting in a word on his behalf, although he was not, as he probably hoped, invited to visit or stay at the Raglans' home, Cefntilla Court near Usk. He went on a number of day trips by rail and cycle before returning to Hereford, and arrived back on the Island just in time for the official farewell to Bishop Straton who had been appointed as Bishop of Newcastle. At Government House pictures were presented by the Governor, an inkstand on behalf of the Mothers' Union by Louisa, and a cheque for episcopal robes by Arthur, all on behalf of the subscribers. In September he interviewed candidates in Leeds for the post of secretary to the Island's Council of Education, then went to Edinburgh for the Pan-Celtic Congress (Chapter 7), and in October to London to take Margery to the British Museum, the National Gallery and the National Portrait Gallery before she set off with two friends to stay with a family in Berlin.

A week or so later the Keys, in a private meeting, unanimously decided to ask the Governor to apply for an honour for Arthur Moore. Nothing came of it, but Moore's colleagues must have been well aware of his poor health and his struggle to continue with his duties. That was why, before he set off to Jamaica in December, he was congratulated on having a holiday, and J. T. Cowell, MHK, wished him a very happy time and 'that you come back from your holiday fully restored to health'. To a friendly correspondent wishing him well, Moore replied, 'Thanks for your very kind letter. I am not ill but somewhat 'run down". If he did know how ill he was, he was not admitting it, perhaps not even to himself.[14]

The holiday lasted two months in all. On 14 December Arthur sailed from Avonmouth on the SS *Port Henderson*, belonging to Elder Dempster's Imperial Direct West India Mail Line, 'a fine old-fashioned ship with a bowsprit, of 5,000 tons'. It was a slow and sometimes rough Atlantic crossing, via the Azores and the Sargasso Sea, where he enjoyed seeing the shoals of flying fish. They arrived at Kingston, Jamaica, on 28 December, thirty-six hours late, after what was said to be the worst passage for years.

Kingston was still showing the effects of the earthquake of 14 January 1906. Ill or not, Arthur's usual zest and curiosity asserted themselves, and he soon made himself at home in colonial society, visiting the Botanical Gardens and the Jamaica Club, where on his second day on the island he succeeded in finding an Old Rugbeian artillery officer, playing golf with a ship's commander, and attending a dance in the evening. On New Year's Eve he visited the camp of the West Indies Regiment, and watched the officers play polo – or even possibly joined them.[15] On 1 January he went on a pony ride, and the following day he felt the shock of an earth tremor. During the ensuing month he succeeded in getting round most of the island, by railway or carriage, including Spanish Town and Montego Bay. He stayed up in the hills, and visited a cattle ranch, a tea estate, a coffee plantation and a magistrates' court. He sat in a rocker on the verandah of an American luxury hotel watching deluges of tropical rain, and met a judge and an American millionaire. He observed that Americans were 'noisy and objectionable in the aggregate', but pleasant individually. He noticed that in church black and white were mixed, not segregated as in the United States. He walked nine miles one day, up a 3,000ft hill. He noticed a number of Jewish Jamaicans, and wondered if they had emigrated in Cromwell's time. He found, among the black population, that 'no one reads or writes'.

Quine's preface to *Nessy Heywood* introduces some fresh material which is not in his notes or in Moore's diaries. 'He ascertained that the negro children are bright and intelligent up to the age of 12 or 13, but beyond that point are generally capable of no further mental development', and more in the same vein. Such racist stereotypes were common a century ago but, again, we do not know whether this was something Moore said in conversation, or whether Quine was attributing his own opinions to Moore.

The holiday seems to have been a huge success, as Arthur Moore's last long holiday abroad on his own. After buying postcards and necklaces, he boarded the SS *Port Kingston* for the return journey on 30 January 1908, and arrived in England on 11 February. England at that time of year was 'ghastly', and he was thrown right into the thick of things; letters awaited him at Bristol with the information that the Home Secretary, Herbert

Gladstone, would see the Keys deputation on constitutional reform at noon on the 13th. He went straight to London and met the other members of the deputation, J. T. Cowell and William Goldsmith, at the Ivanhoe Hotel. On the 12th he had a private conversation in the morning with a Mr Aitken, a official at the Home Office, and with only moderate success tried to find out from him what the Governor and the Legislative Council had been saying against the scheme of constitutional reform. It was a fact that the Council, as well as Lord Raglan, were almost universally opposed to the proposals, and some of them were very hostile to the Keys – especially Arthur Moore's own brothers-in-law. On 6 December 1907 George Ring wrote to Raglan that there was not a single member of the Keys 'who is in any sense capable of leadership, of organising opinion, or of exerting any real influence either inside or outside the House'. Cyril Hughes-Games wrote on 9 December, with all the weighty experience of his thirty-seven years, that 'a steady process of deterioration in the calibre of these members [of the Keys] has been only too noticeable for many years past'. Raglan, who had perhaps encouraged his subordinates to write in this vein, said much the same thing in his covering letter, commenting that from about 1889 the social standing, composition and character of the Keys had been steadily declining.[16]

Moore, Ring and Hughes-Games were all members of a charmed circle of the Island's ruling elite. But what a contrast! Ring and Hughes-Games were, at best, loyal servants of an aristocratic, autocratic Governor, and were committed to supporting his position. At worst they could be seen as self-serving, self-interested and over-paid lackeys. Arthur Moore, on the other hand, was a devoted public servant, committed to maintaining the position of the House of Keys and, unlike most of his social equals in the Island, a genuine liberal and champion of popular representative government. On 13 February: 'A most gratifying interview with Mr Gladstone, who was very cordial. I stated the case for the House and my colleagues added some remarks. We then answered Mr. Gladstone's questions and those of Mr. Samuel, the under-secretary of State, a very shrewd-looking young fellow. The interview lasted an hour and a half altogether'. The Home Office minute of the meeting noted that the Home Secretary said he sympathised with the views of the deputation, which he largely shared. 'He did not doubt there was a general popular feeling in favour of a larger share in government being allotted to elected representatives of the people. He attached no importance to the suggestion that the Island did not contain sufficient competent persons'. However 'he could not at that moment express definite views as to what might be done, or when, as the pressure of work was very great both in the Department, and on the Government as a whole'. [15]

Arthur Moore had done all he could to press for constitutional reform.[17] Meanwhile he had also received, on his arrival in Bristol, a surprising piece of family news. Helen, not quite twenty years old, had become engaged to a Mr Walford, 'a chartered accountant in a good position in the north of England. This was startling news as I did not even know that she was acquainted with him!' At Liverpool on the way home he met Helen and Mr Walford, who had come from Norton where Helen had been staying with Winifred, and where the couple had met. 'I was very pleased with Mr. Walford who seemed very nice, sensible and straightforward and, as his monetary position is quite satisfactory, I have given my consent to the engagement'. He arrived home with Helen after a good crossing, and was delighted to see Louisa and young Arthur both looking much better for their stay at Malvern while he had been away.

On going into Douglas on 17 February Arthur Moore received 'numberless congratulations on my improved appearance'. The next day he was welcomed back to the Keys. While in Jamaica he had sent a postcard to Dalrymple Maitland, the Acting Speaker, saying 'It is lovely and very hot. I am feeling very much better already', and now he was welcomed back 'in renewed health and vigour, well, fit and brown'. He reported on the meeting with the Home Secretary and read out the petition in order to ensure that, for the first time, it was printed in full in the *Proceedings of Tynwald*. But the jubilation about the Speaker's improved health was misjudged. He soon succumbed to a severe attack of influenza, complicated by a touch of pneumonia, and on doctor's orders was kept at home for nearly three weeks.

No further progress was made towards constitutional reform in 1908, because the Home Secretary was too fully occupied with other matters. Nor could Arthur Moore undertake any more energetic bicycle tours. Slowly, from mid-March on, he resumed his public activities, speaking on constitutional reform to the National Union of Teachers, and then, most importantly, successfully pressing the Hospital Committee to accept the offer from Noble's Trustees to build a new hospital on the Hills estate and to endow it with £20,000. At the annual meeting Arthur Moore's proposal from the chair was carried by thirty-seven votes to five, his opponents preferring to build additions to the old hospital. His proposal in Tynwald that Hango Hill be protected at a cost of £250 was also carried.

'Mr Walford', as he was still called, came to stay at Easter, and he and Helen were married at Kirk Braddan in June. The wedding was a low-key event, with none but relatives present, and no reception, because Louisa's mother was dangerously ill. The young couple went off to spend their honeymoon on a motoring tour of Scotland.

Arthur Moore soldiered on as Speaker to the end of the parliamentary session in October, but did not make many speeches. The burning issue of old age pensions, now being introduced in England, attracted much debate, and in July the Keys supported the proposal by sixteen votes to three. But Lord Raglan, predictably, would not take 'a leap into the dark', said he had no idea how the Island could pay for it, and argued for delay.

Moore lacked the energy to maintain his weather observations at Cronkbourne any longer, and transferred his weather station to Douglas Borough Cemetery at the end of May. He continued travelling on Steam Packet business when necessary, but did very little otherwise. He enjoyed another naval visit in August, this time led by Admiral Assheton Curzon-Howe, Commander-in-Chief of the Atlantic Fleet. He managed a trip to London in late September, when he unexpectedly bumped into Helen and 'Dolf' (Adolphus Walford) at the Franco-British exhibition. He saw the Whitakers in Hampshire and the Seckhams at Lichfield during the same trip.

He still got pleasure from antiquarian and archaeological activities. On 6 May, with the Governor, Philip Kermode and others, he viewed excavations at St Trinian's Chapel, Marown. In August the Ancient Monuments Trustees, of whom he was chairman, met there, and he was enthusiastic about some interesting new discoveries – a rudely-carved small cross, perhaps from the eighth century, and a lintel grave. He was furious in November when a vandal carved his initials on the cross, and pleased when the man was caught, prosecuted and fined.

An evocative autumnal outing took place on 21 October. 'Went on interesting expedition with Lord Raglan, John Quine, P. M. C. Kermode and John Crellin to Lag-ny-Keilley, driving over the mountains by Foxdale and the Round Table. The temperature has, at last, dropped considerably so it was cold on the mountains. We walked along the steep slope of Cronk-na-Irey [sic] Lhaa to Lag-ny-Keilley where the old keeill has just been opened out. It is of the usual type and three primitive crosses probably of 7th or 8th century have been found. The sun came out when we got there and we ate our sandwiches amid what is probably the finest rock scenery in the British Isles, except the cliffs at Hoy. We returned via Dalby'.

In November Dr Sharp returned to the Island. He pronounced young Arthur and Margery 'all right ... but in my case there will have to be another operation'. Meanwhile there was another general election in progress, and the three unopposed candidates in Middle, Moore, Maitland, and Clucas – all, as it happened, present or future Speakers of the House of Keys – did the usual round of meetings in Onchan, Braddan and Santon. In Onchan, Arthur Moore reviewed his political activities and opinions. He had presented two reform petitions to two Home Secretaries, and he was in favour of better education and more harbour works, for he thought the visiting industry was still in its infancy. He favoured estate duties, or death duties, the taxation of land values, an end to the sugar tax, and old age pensions. In answer to a questioner, 'he agreed rooks should be reduced, but would require evidence before he would say the same regarding gulls'. In reply to Samuel Norris on the prospects for reform, he could only say that the Home Secretary received them most favourably.[18]

He was unanimously re-elected as Speaker of the new House of Keys on 24 November. At some time in this year he had edited another collection of documents, *Extracts from the Journals of the Self-Elected House of Keys*, covering the years 1762-1826, and 1843 to 1867. But now he faced another severe ordeal, the worst yet. 'December 11th. I underwent an operation by Dr Sharp for the removal of a tumour and polypi at the back of my nose. I was under ether for nearly three hours. The shock of the operation was a considerable one so much so that I am still on the 24th somewhat an invalid'.

From January to March 1909 Arthur Moore was back in the Speaker's chair. The new House of Keys reaffirmed its support for old age pensions by nineteen votes to four in Tynwald, with the Legislative Council and the Governor all against it. Lord Raglan found a new reason for opposition to pensions, that the working classes did not know how old they were.

The weather in March was appallingly cold, and in April Arthur set off on his last foreign expedition, to the Canaries with his daughter Margery. It was described by John Quine as 'a forlorn hope effort after health'. They were away from the Island from 2 to 30 April, sailing from Southampton with the Union Castle line and arriving in Las Palmas, Gran Canaria, on the 9th. They seem to have relied on a family called Quiney. First, a Quiney working in Union Castle's local office introduced them to his brother, who ran Quiney's Hotel in Las Palmas. They saw Good Friday processions, went to a service in the cathedral, and visited a museum. Then they drove twenty miles to the village of Telde, and the next day 1,500 feet higher up to the village of Monte, in fertile countryside, where they stayed at the Bella Vista Hotel, kept by Mr and Mrs Quiney senior. There Arthur Moore collapsed for five days with 'Canary Fever'. They stayed on for another five days, with some day trips and walks, but left the island on the 21st on the SS *Dover Castle*, which stopped briefly at Tenerife to load up with fruit and potatoes. Arriving back in London on the 27th, Arthur went straight to a doctor the next morning, and then took his daughter to a matinée. It was bitterly cold again. On the 29th they went shopping in London, and had a rough passage home from Liverpool. The holiday had not been a success, and they discovered that while they were away young Arthur had had pneumonia. John Quine wrote of Moore, 'When he returned to the Island, we saw that he had come back to die'.

However, 'worn in body but indomitable in spirit', Arthur Moore attended a special meeting of the Keys in private on 1 May, and then went with Maitland to try and persuade the Governor not to increase the duty on spirits and tobacco, or at least not to make it permanent – another forlorn endeavour. On 9 May, 'The return to my ordinary life – walking and meetings – has led to the indigestion becoming much worse. I am therefore condemned to lie down and live on milk for a week'. He did not seem to realise that the 'indigestion' was cancer, and he was ill for the rest of May.

In June came two pieces of good news. First, Arthur and Louisa became grandparents when Helen had a little girl on the 19th. Second, on the 23rd the Home Secretary at last wrote to Lord Raglan saying that his under-secretary, Herbert Samuel, would visit the Island. But almost immediately the visit was cancelled, as Samuel was appointed Chancellor of the Duchy of Lancaster. Due above all to the Great War, it would be another ten years before reform came to the Island.

In July Moore was back in the Keys again, and appeared at St Johns on Tynwald Day to promulgate the new laws in Manx. On 4 July 'Mrs. Field, authoress of a charming book on the Isle of Man, beautifully illustrated by (Donald) Maxwell, came to tea with her publisher, Mr. John Lane. I thought her very nice and him a well-informed interesting man'. The book, *The Isle of Man* by Agnes Herbert, was published in 1909 by the Bodley Head with a foreword by A. W. Moore, one of his last pieces of writing. The author thanked him for his kindly goodwill, letting her use the fruits of his research, and writing the foreword.

On 9 July Moore unveiled a bust of T. E. Brown at a special session of Tynwald in Douglas Town Hall, and gave an appreciation of his old friend. On 12 July he made the last entry in his diary, about the unseasonably cold weather. But Arthur Moore was still an enthusiast with an interest in life, as a remarkable series of thirteen letters and cards written to Sophia Morrison between June and October 1909 make plain.[19] The main subject was their ongoing literary collaboration on what was to be *The Vocabulary of the Anglo-Manx Dialect*. It would eventually be published by Oxford University Press in 1924, with Moore, Morrison and Edmund Goodwin named as the joint authors, and reprinted in 1991. Moore still wrote like a man expecting to recover, in pen if he was up and about, in pencil if he was in bed. On 22 July, 'I have to lie down a good deal and am plagued with numerous meetings etc. Moreover I have undertaken a brief biography of Nessy

Heywood [sister of Peter Heywood of Mutiny on the *Bounty* fame]. A distant relative of hers has discovered some new and interesting material, consisting of poetry and letters by her which have never been published. She was a wonderful girl'. This book, *Nessy Heywood*, was completed and published by subscription by Brown and Sons in 1913, with the oft-quoted preface by John Quine. There is much more in the letters about the *Vocabulary*, which Moore thought would be a very interesting book. He was a courteous and thoughtful collaborator to the end.

On 24 August, 'I am still in bed and am getting very tired of it. My mind seems to get active in proportion to the enforced idleness of my body!' On 12 October he was in the chair at the Keys opening session, and nominated a deputation to the Governor about pensions and taxation. On 16 October, in his last letter to Sophia Morrison, 'I have so much on hand at present, and my health is so feeble that I cannot do very much in the way of literary work'. He managed to attend a Board meeting, and sat next to his colleague Dalrymple Maitland, on 26 October. John Quine, writing in his best vein, said 'It was absolutely pathetic to see business transacted by the House [of Keys], where every member felt for him an intense personal regard, in some cases an intense affection – as intense as was possible, where it was centred on a man so undemonstrative'.

There was a rapid collapse in November. Arthur William Moore died from primary cancer of the stomach at 1.15am on 12 November 1909, at his home, Woodbourne House, Douglas. He was fifty-six years old. The witness, present at the death, who informed the registrar was his sister-in-law Helena Ring.

A. W. Moore died on 12 November 1909 and was buried in Braddan Cemetery three days later; his funeral was described as being one of the largest ever seen on the Island. Here the procession is coming down Alexander Road towards Bray Hill, en route from Woodbourne House to Braddan New Church. The coffin bore an iron cross and a wreath of white flowers from Louisa, but, as was usual at the time, she did not attend. The mourners were led by fourteen-year-old Arthur Hughes-Games Christian Moore.

Chapter 10

AFTERWARDS

Arthur Moore's death, long expected, was followed three days later by a funeral described as one of the largest the Island had ever seen. As was then the custom, his widow Louisa did not attend, and the mourners were led by his son, fourteen-year-old Arthur, for whom this must have been a considerable ordeal. The procession from Woodbourne House to Braddan New Church was hundreds strong, with contingents from the many public bodies with which Moore had been involved, very many friends and private individuals, and spectators lining the route. Most shops in Douglas were closed for a few hours. The ceremony, conducted by Bishop Drury, the vicar and Canon John Quine, as Chaplain of the House of Keys, was simple, orthodox and moving. Burial followed in Braddan Cemetery. In death, Moore attained the status of a national hero.[1] There was only, perhaps, one discordant note – an absence. The Governor, Lord Raglan, sent his carriage, and his secretary as his representative, but did not attend in person as he was indisposed.

Moore's will, made in 1902, was surprisingly perfunctory: he left everything, amount unspecified, to his wife and her heirs, but did not appoint executors. Letters of administration were granted to Louisa Moore, her son-in-law Adolphus Walford of Stockton-on-Tees, her brother Cyril Hughes-Games, advocate, and Thomas Cubbon, secretary of the Isle of Man Bank.[2]

Moore was replaced as Speaker of the House of Keys by his colleague as MHK for Middle, Dalrymple Maitland. In due course the Keys paid their own tribute by commissioning a bust by the Manx sculptor Frank Mowbray Taubman and a painting by the Liverpool Manx artist Robert E. Morrison, both installed in the Keys chamber in 1911.[3]

All this was to be expected, but not what happened next. At the time of the 1891 census a young Cambridge undergraduate, George Frederick Clucas, son of the headmaster of Repton, had been staying on the Island with his uncle the Revd Benjamin Clarke (1831-1903), vicar of Marown. His grandfather, Revd John Thomas Clarke (1799-1888), had married Betsy Clucas in Santon in 1822 and, after her death in 1862, a second wife with the same surname, Catherine Clucas. His father George Petman Clarke (1827-1902) had changed his name to Clucas, presumably for some reason connected with one of these marriages.[4]

In 1894 Clucas qualified for the English Bar, and in 1895 for the Manx Bar. By the time of the 1901 census he was living in Douglas, an advocate aged thirty-one, in lodgings at 19 Burnside Terrace. This is on the west side of Woodbourne Road between Berkeley Street and Albany Street Lane, almost opposite the Moores' home at Woodbourne House.[5] Clucas would have dressed in the correct formal gentlemanly style befitting his profession. In an age when dress was a precise marker of social class, he and the Moores must at least have known each other by sight.

Arthur Moore and Frederick Clucas certainly knew each other by 1903, and probably earlier, through shared antiquarian interests.[6] By 1908 Clucas had moved to Bridgemount at Tromode, close to Cronkbourne, and he entered Manx politics by standing for the Keys as one of the three representatives for Middle, alongside Moore and Maitland. The three men were all elected unopposed, spoke together at a series of meetings in Onchan, Braddan and Santon. Clucas, the young beginner, was also the most radical, enthusiastically endorsing the demands of the Manx Reform League. Samuel Norris, secretary of the League, even signed his nomination papers for the Keys election.[7]

Once in the Keys, Frederick Clucas made a favourable impression on his colleagues as a talented newcomer. In January 1910 he was elected as one of a committee of three MHKs to consider the form of a public memorial to the late Speaker. But on 14 October, when the Keys were not sitting, he suddenly resigned, writing to Speaker Maitland from Repton to say: 'As I have decided to leave the Island and, for the immediate future, to take up my abode with my brother and sister here, I now write to you resigning my seat'. This was strictly true, but misleading insofar as it left the impression that his resignation had to do with family problems in Repton.[8]

Meanwhile, Arthur and Louisa's son Arthur Hughes-Games Moore was removed from King William's College at the end of the summer term, and resumed his education at Clifton College, Bristol, in the autumn of 1910.[9] Presumably his mother had already moved to Bristol, or was in the process of doing so, perhaps with Margery, her unmarried daughter. On 24 January 1911, just fourteen months after Arthur Moore's death, Louisa married George Frederick Clucas, describing himself in English style as a barrister, by special licence at St Matthew's Parish Church, Kingsdown, Bristol.[10]

It seems overwhelmingly likely that Clucas' resignation from the Keys, the transfer of young Arthur to Clifton, and the move from the Island to

Bristol, were all motivated by the couple's desire to marry quickly and to set up house in a place where their history was not known.

Once it became known, this speedy remarriage of Arthur Moore's widow must have shocked public opinion in the Island, and no doubt the circumstances surrounding the marriage were the subject of lively speculation. A story widely circulated since is that Louisa and Clucas had been childhood sweethearts but, whatever the origins of this myth, it seems virtually impossible that it could be true. In the first place, Louisa was born on 13 August 1864, Clucas not until 1870. It is not usual for young women to be attracted to boys five or six years younger than themselves. At the time of Louisa's marriage to Arthur Moore she was twenty-two, Clucas only sixteen or seventeen. He was not even living in the Isle of Man, but was a schoolboy at Repton, the Derbyshire public school where his father was headmaster. One of the odder things that Louisa and her new husband had in common was that they both came from families whose surname had changed. Louisa Hughes-Games' father had been born Jones. Frederick Clucas had Manx origins, but his father had been born Clarke. Their fathers, incidentally, were also both clergymen who had been headmasters.

On the day she married Frederick Clucas in January 1911 Louisa was living at Cotham Lodge, Cotham Park, Bristol. Clucas gave his address as Repton, Derbyshire. He was forty or forty-one, and Louisa was forty-six; the disparity in their ages was concealed by an evasive statement on the marriage certificate: 'Both of full age'. They had not done anything immoral or illegal in rushing into matrimony so soon after Arthur Moore's death, but Louisa had acted in a way which some people might have considered disloyal to his memory; had they remained in the Island, the couple could well have found themselves facing obloquy and ostracism. Clucas came back during the Keys election of 1913, not in order to stand himself but to support pro-reform candidates, and perhaps to keep his name before the public.[11] He and Louisa continued to live in England until after the Great War; during the war Clucas held an important position in London as deputy director at the Ministry of Munitions.

The reactions of the Moore and Hughes-Games families to the marriage of Louisa to Frederick Clucas can only be guessed at. Hannah Moore outlived her son by five years, dying in November 1914. She had not altered the will she made in 1909 after Arthur's death; at that time she clearly wanted Louisa to move to Cronkbourne, which in any case she would have inherited as Arthur's widow.[12] The legalities were complicated, and the Great War had altered social mores in an utterly unforeseen way. In the end, after substantial payments of £3,000 or £4,000 had been made to each of

Arthur's unmarried sisters, the Clucases moved into Cronkbourne (which had been shut up during the war) in 1919 or 1920. Louisa's brother Cyril, the Vicar-General, and her brother-in-law George Ring, Attorney General, cannot have been happy about Clucas' radicalism.

For those who cherished the memory of Arthur Moore, the ironies of the situation must have been very apparent. Moore had loved Cronkbourne all his life, had always thought of it as his real home, and had no doubt confidently expected to inherit when his mother died. But he had not lived there since 1887, and in the end the prize had eluded him. Now Louisa could at last enjoy being the mistress of Cronkbourne, but with a new husband by her side. This husband was also, like Moore, a public school man and a Cambridge graduate with antiquarian interests.

What is more, Frederick Clucas was re-elected to the Keys in 1919 and in the same year, after little more than two years in total in the Keys, was elected as Speaker. The post-war political mood in the Island was overwhelmingly in favour of change and reform, and against the pre-war status quo, and Clucas was the man of the hour. He remained Speaker until his death in 1937, having outstripped Arthur Moore's period in the office by eighteen years to eleven. The Clucases even arranged another royal visit, although not by such an illustrious visitor as King Edward VII: Prince George of Kent put in an appearance on the lawns of Cronkbourne in 1932, an event which was duly commemorated, like the earlier royal visit, by an inscription carved on the fireplace in the hall, and memorialised in a family scrapbook.[13]

Louisa had achieved a remarkable social success, being the only woman ever to have been married to two different Speakers of the House of Keys. And the Clucases' final triumph occurred in 1937, when Frederick Clucas was awarded the knighthood which Arthur Moore had coveted, and Louisa became Lady Clucas.

But they did not have long to enjoy their new status. In November that year Sir Frederick Clucas developed peritonitis, and died in Noble's Hospital aged sixty-seven. Louisa, who had been at his bedside, collapsed with a heart attack brought on by the shock and died just a few hours later, on the same day, aged seventy-three. As the memorial plaque in Braddan Church, where their joint funeral was held, says: 'In their deaths they were not divided'. But in their burial places, they were. After the funeral service two corteges left the church, going in different directions. Perhaps at the insistence of Arthur Moore's children and sisters, Louisa was buried in the same plot as her first husband in Braddan Cemetery, the body of her three-month-old son William exhumed from the grave of his Aunt Florence and interred with them. Sir Frederick Clucas joined his ancestors in Santon Churchyard.[14]

The Keys commemorated their illustrious Speaker by commissioning a portrait by Robert E. Morrison, a highly successful artist who was also President of the Liverpool Manx Society, and a marble bust by the London-based Manx sculptor Frank Mowbray Taubman. Both were unveiled in 1911.

This was now the end, after 110 years, of the Moores and Clucases at Cronkbourne. Arthur Hughes-Games Christian Moore, now a man of forty-two, was living in England with his family and working as a land agent. Neither he nor anyone else in the Moore family could afford to live at Cronkbourne any longer. The house was shut up again, and after the Second World War it was sold out of the family. The selling-off of inherited country houses had been a widespread trend in Britain during the inter-war depression; at least Cronkbourne escaped the common fate of demolition.

Several of Arthur Moore's siblings remained in the Island, or returned in retirement; some of them have memorials in Braddan Church. Arthur himself has a stained glass window and a plaque dedicated to his memory; the biblical text is 'But the path of the just is as the shining light that shineth more and more unto the perfect day' (Proverbs, Chapter IV, verse 18). The last of his siblings to die was the youngest, Katie Mildred Moore (1874-1958), who also has a plaque in her memory. She outlived her illustrious elder brother by nearly fifty years.

As for Arthur and Louisa's children, Helena Walford died in 1969; her sister Margery, who also has a memorial plaque at Braddan, married Colonel Edward Bradley, Deputy Lord Lieutenant of Lancashire, and died in 1965. A. W. Moore's son 'Arthur Hughes-Games Christian Moore, M.A., J.P., of Cronkbourne', as his memorial inscription describes him, returned with his wife Olive to live in the Island in his retirement, first at Baldrine and then at a house called The Moorings in Eleanora Drive, Douglas. He died in 1972, the last of this particular Moore family to live in the Isle of Man. The family continues to flourish elsewhere.

The fate of A. W. Moore's books and papers was linked to the disposal of Cronkbourne and the dispersal of the Moore family. At the time of his death Moore owned the finest collection of Manx books and manuscripts in the Island. Whether these were kept at Woodbourne House or Cronkbourne is not known; possibly the latter, since his father had also collected Manx books, and the prefaces to all his own books are signed 'A. W. Moore, Cronkbourne', as though they had been written there. He must have assumed that his collection would remain intact at Cronkbourne in perpetuity.

Moore was a meticulous preserver of letters and manuscripts. In this he resembled his uncle the Archdeacon who, as Moore tells us in his diary for 1886, 'had kept not only most of the letters he had ever received, but also his answers to them'. But, immediately after the Archdeacon's funeral, 'we stayed several days arranging things, tearing up letters etc'. The practical imperatives of house clearance are often the most important consideration for relatives after a death in the family. Additionally, many Victorians felt that it was an improper intrusion into privacy to preserve and read the correspondence and private papers of the dead. Arthur Moore's letter books (which included, for example, all his letters from Lord Loch, as he wrote in his diary in 1900) could well have suffered the same fate as his uncle's.

Moore may himself have ordered the records of the family firm to be destroyed; the business was for him a matter of duty rather than pleasure. He would probably not have found its records interesting or, at a time before business history had been thought of, been able to imagine that anyone else would find them interesting in the future.

But what about the missing travel diaries? Moore refers to them often in his main diaries, and it is clear to any reader of the preface to *Nessy Heywood* that John Quine had used all the diaries, both domestic and travel, in preparing his account of Moore's life, written in 1912 and published in 1913. This is confirmed by Quine's notes, recently acquired by the Manx National Heritage Library. It seems likely that Quine borrowed the travel diaries, which he evidently scrutinised in detail, but never returned them. By the time he wrote his account Louisa was living in Bristol and no doubt more concerned with her new husband than with chasing after diaries borrowed from the old one. There is evidence that Quine had a tendency to collect and hang onto other people's documents: the manuscript book in which he made his notes on Moore's diaries also includes a draft letter of February 1912, in reply to a Peel solicitor called Hodgson, concerning Quine's retention of notes belonging to Mr Goodwin, presumably Edmund Goodwin of Peel (1845-1925).[15] According to oral tradition within the Quine family, many manuscripts and papers that Quine left on his death in 1940 were carefully hoarded by his son, Commander John Lindsay Quine, who put them beneath the floor of his house, The Spinney at Baldrine, for safekeeping – where they rotted away.[16] We cannot be sure, but this was perhaps the likely fate of Arthur Moore's travel diaries.

By the time Moore's surviving papers were handed over to the Manx Museum Library in 1938, nearly thirty years had elapsed since his death. And there were still some of his books, including finely bound prizes from the 1870s, in the attics of Cronkbourne after the Second World War.[17] It was due to good fortune, and also to the generosity of Arthur Moore the younger, that in 1938 the Manx Museum, on behalf of the Manx people, was able to take into public ownership a substantial amount of miscell-aneous printed and manuscript material, including the surviving diaries. Most of it had to do with Manx history, and much of it had constituted the raw material of Moore's publications.

On the centenary of A. W. Moore's death, he remains a key figure in the history of Manx culture. His books are still read and consulted, the form of immortality every writer aspires to. The preceding pages have, it is hoped, given some idea of the size of his contribution to our knowledge of the Isle of Man's past.

His part in public life also deserves to be remembered. Cautious but liberal-minded, he inherited his father's strong sense of duty and integrity. As Speaker, he maintained the rights of the House of Keys, and set an example for his successors to follow. He did his best to secure democratic reform in the Island, even if it was not achieved in his lifetime.

He showed zest and energy in everything he did, including his travels and recreations. Among the many tributes to him, three are worth recalling. Caesar Cashin, Peel fisherman and Manx Gaelic speaker, said cryptically when he heard of Moore's death, 'The band is off the sheaf'.[18] The Trustees of Ancient Monuments remembered him as a personal friend of them all, with his genial manner and constant courtesy.[19] And Lord Raglan, though he did not attend his funeral, unveiled his bust in the House of Keys in 1911, and said simply 'I loved Arthur Moore'.[20]

Appendix I

THE GENEALOGY OF THE MOORE FAMILY OF DOUGLAS AND CRONKBOURNE

The Moores, like many Manx families, have taken great interest in establishing their family history and lines of ancestral descent, a task complicated by Moore being such a common surname in the Island, with several unconnected Moore families. A. W. Moore was deeply interested in his family origins; though he never published a book on the subject, he worked out a family tree in about 1881 and incorporated it in his first substantial piece of research , 'Old Manx Families' (MNHL microfilm RC3).

His grandson A. R. W. Moore did extensive genealogical research in the 1950s in the then Manx Record Office (known later as General Registry), with the assistance of W. R. Serjeant, the first professional archivist at the Manx Museum Library (letter from A. R. W. Moore to Nigel Crowe, 31 December 1982). This work bore fruit in A. R. W. Moore's typescript history, 'An Account of the Family of the Moores of More Hall-Bank Hall and of Pulrose-Cronkbourne' (MNHL MS 12504). As this title asserts, the Moores of Cronkbourne believed that they were descended both from the Moores of More Hall and Bank Hall near Liverpool, a Lancashire county family which can be traced back to mediaeval times, and from the Moores of Pulrose on the outskirts of Douglas, a substantial landed estate from the sixteenth century on.

However Nigel Crowe – a more recent genealogist and himself a descendant of one branch of the Douglas Moores – has cast doubt on both these claims. See Nigel G. Crowe, 'The Moores of Ballakilley, Marown', in *Proceedings of the Isle of Man Natural History and Antiquarian Society*, Vol. X, No. 4, 1994, 17-40. Table 3, 'Edward Moore of Douglas and his Issue' provides a family tree which includes the eighteenth century clergyman Revd Edward Moore, Vicar General (1696-1751), and his brother Revd Philip Moore (1709-83), and also a long line of merchants and tradesmen, beginning with Edward Moore, a Douglas glover who died in 1667, and culminating in James Moore (1772-1846), linen manufacturer of Douglas and Tromode, A. W. Moore's grandfather.

The implication is that at some point in the family's history the Moores of Douglas and Tromode/Cronkbourne indulged in wishful thinking in order to elevate the social status of their putative ancestors, and perhaps to support the adoption of a family coat of arms by James Moore. Be that as it may, it is indisputable that by the time of A. W. Moore's birth the family were, whatever their pedigree, not only industrial magnates but also generally recognised as landed gentry.[1]

I am grateful to Nigel Crowe for discussing this subject with me, and also for lending me the file of correspondence between himself and the late A. R. W. Moore, A. W. Moore's grandson.

A. W. Moore's bookplate, displaying the 'family arms'. A. R. W. Moore claimed in his 1950s account of the family that this had been 'granted' to James Moore, but there is no such record at the College of Arms. In his family entry in *Old Manx Families* A. W. Moore described the achievement:

Arms: *Three hounds, courant, in a pale argent.*
Crest: *A moor-fowl proper, guttée de poix, argent.*
Motto: *Dieu et mon Fort.*

Heraldically speaking, this is a garbled description. The use of coats of arms without authority has been common practice for centuries, and continues today.

Appendix II

ARTHUR MOORE AND THE DRINKWATERS OF KIRBY

Arthur Moore's friendship with the Drinkwater family was lifelong. Such old family friendships can assume a character of permanence and inevitability to those involved, so that most of the time they are taken for granted, occasion little comment, and can therefore become almost invisible to the biographer. Yet there is enough information about the Drinkwaters in Moore's diary to provide at least a superficial impression of the friendship. There is also a recently written, unpublished, Drinkwater family history which has been deposited in the Manx National Heritage Library, together with twenty-five boxes of the family papers.[1]

Kirby, which is still the Drinkwater family home, is a large thirteen-bedroomed Georgian mansion, built between 1813 and 1818 for Colonel Mark Wilks who was for several years the Governor of St Helena, and thus chief gaoler of the deposed Emperor Napoleon Bonaparte. After Colonel Wilks' death the Drinkwaters, an energetic family of Liverpool merchants, moved in, initially as tenants, in 1835, and as owners from 1840.

The Moores of Cronkbourne, only a mile or so away, and also on the outskirts of Douglas (Kirby with the Dhoo running through its grounds, and Cronkbourne on the Glass), were among the nearest neighbours of similar social standing. William Leece Drinkwater, a lawyer, came to live in the Island as Deemster in 1847, inherited Kirby from an uncle in 1850, and retired after fifty years in 1897. Described as 'a devoted Churchman and loyalist', he served ex officio on the Legislative Council and was chairman of the Lunatic Asylum Committee which oversaw the building of Ballamona Hospital.[2] He and his wife were well known to Arthur throughout his childhood. After four daughters they had two sons, George, born in 1852, and John, born in 1854, who were natural playmates for Arthur, born in 1853.

Thus Arthur remembered that when he first heard of the death of Prince Albert in 1861, he was at a children's party at Kirby, aged eight, and that three years later he fought George Drinkwater, taking up the cudgels in defence of George's younger brother John.

In 1871 the three boys all took part in the Public Schools Shooting

Competition at Wimbledon, George shooting for Eton, John for Cheltenham and Arthur for Rugby. It was the same summer that Arthur spent ten days in August on holiday shooting game at Roddam Hall, Northumberland; the family who lived there were connections by marriage of the Drinkwaters. George went up to Trinity College, Cambridge, in 1871, a year before Arthur, so they must have seen each other there even if they were not close friends. Quine's notes mention that in the summer term of 1873 Arthur took George to his rooms in Master's Court.

John Drinkwater went straight into business in Liverpool after leaving school, and then from 1876 to 1878 worked in a branch office in Valparaiso, Chile. He returned to England early in 1879 to claim an inheritance, and in connection with this – perhaps as a condition of inheriting – changed his name to John Drinkwater Lawe. From 1879 to 1882 he took a degree at Cambridge, and then began to read for the Bar in London, as had George. But by 1883 his health was giving cause for concern. He suffered from shaking and twitching, nervousness, absent-mindedness and an inability to concentrate, and could not pass his legal exams. By May 1884 he was showing strong signs of mental derangement, including delusions, and was taken to St Andrew's Hospital, Northampton, the same institution in which Arthur Moore's younger brother Harry was already living. His brother George denied that he had syphilis, but it must have been a possibility.[3]

Arthur was concerned about his friend's illness. In June 1885, while in London, he went to see John, who was staying at Bourne Hill near Horsham, Sussex. 'He met me at Horsham station with the pony phaeton. He looked well, but rather nervous'. In December George Drinkwater was also seriously ill, in London with congestion of the lungs, but he recovered, as Arthur recorded in his diary.

In 1886 John Drinkwater Lawe seems to have been back at Kirby, certainly by the end of October when Arthur Moore had lunch with him and thought he was 'much better'. Entertainments during that summer for which Moore had been invited to Kirby included rook shooting, and tennis with Volunteer officers camping at Pulrose.

When Arthur was married in February 1887, he received wedding presents from Deemster and Lady Drinkwater (a travelling clock), George and his wife (two small tables), and Mr & Mrs Peter Bourne Drinkwater, an uncle and aunt of the brothers (a brass and silver inkstand and candlesticks). John Lawe gave the newly-married couple very generous gifts, a diamond and pearl brooch for Louisa and a silver breakfast dish for Arthur. In July there was tennis at Kirby again, and in November John came to lunch at Woodburn Place.

A year later, on 10 November 1888, 'My old friend John Drinkwater Lawe died, mercifully, without pain. He was buried privately on the 14th, I being the only one outside the family who was asked to be there'. On the 26th George came over to see Arthur and to tell him that 'John had desired I should have some remembrance of him so they are giving me his cricket bat, pads etc., Hare's *Walks in Rome*, and a small jar'.

The family tragedy probably strengthened existing links between Moore and the Drinkwaters. In 1889 and 1890 the Moores met the George Drinkwaters at several dinner parties, their own and other people's. George, like Arthur, was now a busy public servant in the Island: in August 1889 he was appointed Crown Receiver and Seneschal. Naturally, Arthur and Louisa were at the large garden party held at Kirby in August 1890 to celebrate Deemster and Lady Drinkwater's Golden Wedding.

When Arthur Moore was elected as Speaker of the House of Keys in December 1898, he received an especially warm letter of congratulation from Sir William. Referring to Arthur as 'one whom I have known intimately since his infancy and whom I esteem so highly', the Deemster wrote 'You have in every way – by your high character – your learning – your love of the Island and its institutions – your experience as a Member proved yourself worthy of this very high Honour...'[4] Several further dinner parties at Kirby were recorded in Moore's diary. In December 1901 'Old Deemster D. who will be 90 in March was in wonderfully good form'. On 12 May 1909, six months before his own death, Arthur Moore recorded the death of Sir William at the age of ninety-seven, 'He was a very kind and good friend to me'.

Appendix III

MAIN PUBLICATIONS OF A.W. MOORE

1885-7: *The Manx Note Book* (ed.): quarterly journal, twelve issues bound in three volumes.

1890: *Surnames and Place-names of the Isle of Man.* Preface by John Rhys.

1891: *The Folklore of the Isle of Man.*

Carvallyn Gailckagh: Manx Carvals, (ed., and translated) with J. C. Fargher, R. E. Christian and W. J. Cain.

1893: *Diocesan History of Sodor and Man.*

1893-4: *Bishop Phillips' Manx Prayer Book*, (ed., with John Rhys), two vols.

1896: *Manx Ballads & Music.* Preface by T. E. Brown. In Manx and English.

1897: 'The Physical Anthropology of the Isle of Man', with John Beddoe, in *The Manx Note Book*, Vol. III.

1900: *A History of the Isle of Man.* Two vols.

1901: *Manx Worthies.*

The Story of the Isle of Man: An Historical Reader for Manx Schools.

1904: *An Historical Account of the Isle of Man Steam Packet Company 1830-1904.*

Douglas 100 Years Ago (ed.).

1905: *Notes and Documents from the Records of the Isle of Man* (ed.).

1906: *The Letters of Bishop Hildesley 1755-1772* (ed.).

1908: *Extracts from the Journals of the Self-Elected House of Keys*, 1762-1826, 1843-1867 (ed.).

1913: (posthumous): *Nessy Heywood.* Preface by Revd John Quine.

1924: (posthumous): *A Vocabulary of the Anglo-Manx Dialect*, with Sophia Morrison and Edmund Goodwin (reprinted 1991).

PAPERS GIVEN BY A. W. MOORE TO THE ISLE OF MAN NATURAL HISTORY AND ANTIQUARIAN SOCIETY

1883: Causes of Winds and Storms.

1885: Notes on a Sepulchral Urn, at Port-e-Chee.

1887: The Crucifix Recently Uncovered in the East End of Braddan Old Church.
Manx Literature.
An Historical Sketch of the Manx Language.

1888: The Climate of the Isle of Man.

1890: The Military Organisation of the Isle of Man.

1891: Origin and History of the House of Keys.
Quakers in the Isle of Man and their Treatment.
Notes on the International Folklore Congress.
The Cup of Ballafletcher.

1892: An Ancient MS Account of the Parish of Marown.
The Early Land System of the Isle of Man.

1893: Presidential Address.
The Arms of Man.

1894: Has Climate Changed?

1895: Notes on the Triglot Dictionary.
Foreign Elements in the Manx Language.

1897: Report of Delegate to the British Association Meeting at Liverpool, October 1896.
List of the principal papers at Knowsley relating to the Isle of Man, compiled in September 1896 by A. W. Moore and P. M. C. Kermode, with a further list by A. W. Moore.
Folk Medicine in the Isle of Man.

1899: The Treen Chapels of Marown.
Cup Markings in the Isle of Man.

1902: Children's Rhyming Games in the Isle of Man.
The Ronaldsway Estate.

1903: The Northern Manx and the Southern Manx Volunteers.

1904: Some Notes on the Royal Manx Fencibles.

1906: Tynwald.

1908: The Climate of the Isle of Man.

Appendix IV

THE LITERARY TASTES OF A. W. MOORE

Arthur Moore made this statement to John Quine, probably at the end of 1905:

'Reading is my greatest hobby. From childhood on I have been an omnivorous reader. Earliest books were 'The Ball I live on', 'Near home' and 'Far off'. Allegories had a great effect on my mind. I remember reading *Pilgrim's Progress* at a very early age. I had read all Scott's novels before I was 12, also Macaulay's *History of England*. History has always had a great fascination for me, and I have read more of it than of any other subject. Metaphysical studies never interested me, and even Political Economy was read with some effort. From Sir Walter Scott to Dickens, Thackeray, George Eliot, I have read all the best novels and a good many indifferent ones also! George Eliot's books, which were read as they came out, produced the most marked effect on my mind. Shakespeare has of course a place apart. Otherwise I have always cared for Tennyson much more than any other poetry. Byron comes next in my estimation, then Keats and Shelley. Milton, Dryden, Pope, Wordsworth and Browning I cannot read. With the exception of Tom Brown and Calverley, no poetry written since Tennyson interests me at all. I do not care for obscurity in writing: hence both Browning and George Meredith irritate me! I may say my other greatest hobby is travelling, as its more special objects the study of architecture and pictures'.

Moore read some novels which were more recent than the mid-Victorian classics. A reference in Quine's notes on his tour of Dorset in 1907 shows that he had read Thomas Hardy's *Tess of the d'Urbervilles* (1891), then considered by many people a scandalous book.

REFERENCES

Notes 2 and 3 to the Preface identify the main sources of this book. It would be tedious to note every reference to them. I have therefore, from Chapter 2 onwards, excluded the Moore diaries and the Quine papers from these references.

PREFACE (pages 9-10)

1 John Belchem, 'The Little Manx Nation: Antiquarianism, Ethnic Identity, and Home Rule Politics in the Isle of Man, 1880-1918', *Journal of British Studies*, 2000, 221.
2 Manx National Heritage Library (MNHL), MS 167^{A}, A. W. Moore, 'Diary of events, public and domestic, 1811-1892'; MS 168^{A}, Personal Diary 1892-1909.
3 MNHL MS 11835, John Quine papers. The first biographical account of A. W. Moore is John Quine's preface to Moore's posthumously-published book *Nessy Heywood*, Douglas, 1913, vii-xxvi.
4 Further comments on Moore's writings are to be found in my lecture 'A. W. Moore Revisited', in *Proceedings of the Isle of Man Natural History and Antiquarian Society*, Vol. XII No. 2, forthcoming 2010.
5 John Quine op. cit.
6 *The Manx Note Book*, October 1885, 136.

Chapter 1 (CHILDHOOD, pages 11-20)

1 Annie Cowin, who was probably sixteen when she took up her post as a living-in domestic servant, was a native of Braddan parish and a faithful family retainer who never married. In the censuses of 1861, 1871 and 1881 she is recorded as 'nurse' or 'head nurse' In 1891, 1901 and 1911, when there were no longer any children at Cronkbourne, she had attained the rank of 'lady's maid', probably waiting on Hannah Moore, Arthur's mother. In 1911 she was seventy; no other servant of the Moores remained with the family for so long. Hannah Moore, when she died in 1914, left Annie £100 in her will.
2 These and other childhood memories were recorded by John Quine (MNHL MS. 11835) in a section of his notes headed 'From Diary of A. W. Moore'. But there is no evidence that Moore was a diarist before 1885, let alone as a child. These notes probably resulted from conversations begun in 1898, when Moore became Speaker, as Annie Cowin is referred to as 'still at Cronkbourne 1898!' Quine, perhaps considering such memories as trivial, did not include them in his preface to *Nessy Heywood*.
3 For the earlier history of the Moore family, see Appendix I, The Genealogy of the Moores of Douglas and Cronkbourne (page 155).

4 Katherine A. Forrest, *Manx Recollections: memorials of Eleanor Elliott*, 1894. The author was born in 1847, so must have been relying on hearsay.

5 Since 1810 the Moores had owned bleaching and drying fields at Tromode, following their purchase of Springfield Cottage and adjacent land from the Taubmans. The purchase of the Ballafletcher estate, including a substantial house on the Cronkbourne site, was not formalised until 1829. Information from a talk given by Peter Kelly to the Isle of Man Victorian Society at Cronkbourne, 19 July 2009.

6 A. R.W. Moore, 'An Account of the Family of the Moores of More Hall-Bank Hall and Pulrose-Cronkbourne' (MNHL MS 12504) says that a family coat of arms 'was granted' to James Moore, but this is highly dubious. See Appendix I (page 155). The College of Arms has given the information that 'no person of the name James Moore, resident in the Isle of Man, was granted arms in the 19th century ... however ... the College holds a pedigree of Moore of Douglas, including the aforesaid James Moore. It is an extensive, eleven-generation, pedigree beginning in the 1640s and continuing to the 1960s... The adoption of arms without authority, even by well established and wealthy families, dates back well before the 19th century. Coats of arms do not belong to surnames, but are granted or confirmed to individuals; the right to such arms passes to all descendants of the grantee in the legitimate male line'. Jeremy Goldsmith, research assistant to Rouge Dragon Pursuivant, in email correspondence with Valerie Cottle, 15 and 16 July 2009.

7 L. S. Garrad et al., *The Industrial Archaeology of the Isle of Man*, Newton Abbot, 1972, 126, 200-202, illustrates and discusses Cronkbourne Village, and also mentions the SS *Great Britain*, 172. For an illustration of the *Great Britain*'s maiden voyage, using both steam and sails, see L. T. C. Rolt, *Isambard Kingdom Brunel*, Longmans Green, 1957, and Pelican paperback, 1970, Plate 17.

8 William Fine Moore, 'My Schooldays', MNHL MS 184C.

9 Mrs Hicks Beach, *The Yesterdays Behind the Door*, Liverpool University Press, 1956, 229.

10 For brief sketches of Joseph and William Moore, see A. W. Moore, *Manx Worthies*, Douglas 1901, reprinted 1929 and 1971, 39-40, 77-8. Moore insisted that he had only included his father and uncle in the book 'by wish of the publishers', S. K. Broadbent & Co., footnote to page 9.

11 Quine, 'How Arthur Moore got to be Speaker of the House of Keys', MNHL 11835.

12 I owe the details of Harry Moore's hospital record (obtained with the permission of William Moore, next of kin) to Bobbie Judd, Archives Manager, St Andrew's Healthcare; letter of 20 July 2009 to author.

Chapter 2 (EDUCATION, pages 21-24)

1 Canon John Gelling, *A History of the Manx Church 1698-1911*, Manx Heritage Foundation, 1998, 143, 221.

2 For McBurney's, see Hinton Bird, *An Island That Led: The History of Manx Education*, Port St Mary, Vol. 1, n.d., 170-71, Vol. 2, 1995, 70-71. For Pleignier, see Michael Hoy, *A Blessing to this Island: The Story of King William's College*, 2006.

3 Katherine Forrest, *Manx Recollections*, 105-7, 115-18. Philip Elliott died at the age of twenty-three.
4 For John Pearson and his family, see *Oxford Dictionary of National Biography*, 2004.
5 See entries for Ewan and (Joseph) Henry Christian in Dollin Kelly (ed.), *New Manx Worthies*, Manx Heritage Foundation, 2006, 76-79.
6 For Bishop Drury, see Gelling, *A History of the Manx Church*, 214-15.
7 The previous two paragraphs draw upon *The Meteor*, the Rugby School magazine, which I consulted in the Temple Library with the help of the school archivist, Rusty Maclean.
8 For Frederick Temple, see *Oxford DNB*, also J. B. Hope Simpson, *Rugby since Arnold: A History of Rugby School from 1842*, Macmillan, 1967.
9 Entry for James Maurice Wilson in *Oxford DNB*, and James M. Wilson, *An Autobiography 1836-1931*, A. T. and J. S. Wilson (eds.), Sidgwick and Jackson, 1932.
10 *Oxford DNB* has entries for both Arthur and Henry Sidgwick. See also Noel Annan's seminal essay 'The Intellectual Aristocracy' in J. H. Plumb (ed.), *Studies in Social History: Essays for G. M. Trevelyan*, 1955, 241-87, reprinted in Noel Annan, The Dons, HarperCollins, 1999, paperback 2000, 304-41.
11 For Arthur Sidgwick's homosexuality, see Sheldon Rothblatt, *The Revolution of the Dons*, Faber and Faber, 1968, and Phyllis Grosskurth, *The Life of John Addington Symonds*, Longmans 1974.
12 Information on the Magpie and Stump debating society: telephone conversation between the author and Adam C. Green, deputy archivist, Trinity College, Cambridge.
13 For the previous two paragraphs see Rothblatt, op. cit.; *Oxford DNB* entry on Sir John Robert Seeley; John Kenyon, *The History Men*, Weidenfeld and Nicolson, 2nd edition, 1993, 176-81; Deborah Wormell, *Sir John Seeley and the Uses of History*, Cambridge University Press, 1980.
14 Ian Ousby (ed.), *Cambridge Companion to Literature in English*, revised p/b edition, Cambridge University Press, 1992, 918.
15 Kenyon, op. cit.

Chapter 3 (YOUNG MAN, pages 25-44)

1 W. F. Moore, 'My Schooldays', MNHL MS 184C.
2 *Isle of Man Times*, 24 and 31 March 1877; *Mona's Herald*, 28 March 1877.
3 For Loch, see Derek Winterbottom, *Governors of the Isle of Man Since 1765*, Manx Heritage Foundation, 1999, 63-96. Also see entry on Loch in Dollin Kelly (ed.), *New Manx Worthies*, Manx Heritage Foundation, 2006, 286-9.,
4 Rough calculations from 1881 census of Cronkbourne Village.
5 L. S. Garrad et al., op. cit., Appendix 3, 240-4.
6 L. S. Garrad, op.cit., 172.
7 Mrs Hicks Beach, op. cit., 223, alerted me to this connection, but wrongly identifies Caroline as the wife of Ewan Christian. See 1891 census for Henry and Caroline Christian, 18 Devonshire Place, Marylebone, London.
8 *Manx Quarterly*, No. 1, February 1907, 75-6.
9 For a lively account of riverboat travel at about this time, see Mark Twain, *Life on the Mississippi* (1883).
10 Information from www.closebrothers.co.uk/History, accessed 13 March 2009.

11 See Jane Kidd, *Gilbeys: Wine and Horses*, Lutterworth Press, Cambridge, 1997, for additional information on the Gold family.

Chapter 4 (FAMILY MAN, pages 49-68)

1 For Joshua Hughes-Games, see Canon John Gelling, *A History of the Manx Church*, 1998, 233; for his time at King William's College, see Michael Hoy, *A Blessing to this Island*, 2006, 36-48.
2 The house at Woodburn Place has recently been demolished; it stood on the site of the new Maples Apartments. See 1891 census, and Stuart Slack, *Streets of Douglas – Old and New*, Douglas, 1996, 173.
3 The fullest account is in the *Isle of Man Times*, 26 February 1887. See also *Mona's Herald*, 23 February, and *Manx Sun*, 26 February 1887.
4 Neither of the servants named was still there for the 1891 census (when the Moores and their two daughters were sharing the house with a cook, a housemaid and a nurse).
5 *Mona's Herald*, 18, 25 January, 25 April 1888.
6 Woodbourne House, built *c.*1800, still stands, but it has been absorbed into the Masonic Temple in Woodbourne Road.
7 Contrary to Moore's entry in the *Oxford DNB*, he was not a correspondent of Lord Randolph Churchill. That was another A. W. Moore, Adolphus Warburton Moore (1841-87), private secretary to Lord Randolph and Alpine climber.
8 *Isle of Man Examiner*, 28 April 1894.
9 W. F. Moore's will, MNHL JGS 1895/221.
10 For Harry Wood (1868-1938), see entry in *New Manx Worthies*, 466-8.

Chapter 5 (AUTHOR, pages 69-82)

1 MNHL, microfilm RC3.
2 See Appendix I (page 55).
3 *Transactions of IoMNHAS*, Vol. I, 1879-1884, and *Yn Lioar Manninagh* 1885-1910 are the source of this information. For P. M. C. Kermode, see *New Manx Worthies*, 247-50.
4 For the general background and context of such societies as the IoMNHAS, see David Elliston Allen, *The Naturalist in Britain: A Social History*, Allen Lane 1976, Penguin 1978, and Philippa Levine, *The Amateur and the Professional: Antiquarians, Historians and Archaeologists in Victorian England 1838-1886*, Cambridge University Press, 1986.
5 See Appendix III (page 161).
6 T. E. Brown to Revd Frederick La Mothe, 5 October 1885, in Andrew Graham Dakyns and Belinda Robinson (eds.) *Newly Discovered Letters of T. E. Brown*, Manx Heritage Foundation, 2004, 121.
7 For John Quirk (1800-1885), see also A. W. Moore, *Manx Worthies*, 1901, 105-6.
8 Beddoe, Boyd Dawkins, Rhys and Vigfusson are all included in the *Oxford DNB.*
9 See introduction, 'The Outlines of the Phonology of Manx Gaelic', by John Rhys, to A. W. Moore and John Rhys (eds.), *The Book of Common Prayer in Manx Gaelic*, Manx Society and Oxford University Press, Vol. 2, 1895.
10 For J. J. Kneen (1873-1938) see *New Manx Worthies*, 273-4. The definitive account of Manx place-names is George Broderick, *Place-Names of the Isle of Man* (7 vols.), Tübingen, 1994-2005. See also his shorter *Dictionary of Manx Place-Names*, 2006.
11 For details of the publication and collaborators, see William Cubbon, *Bibliography of*

the Isle of Man, Volume II, 1939. For comment on John Quirk, see *Manx Worthies*, 105; for R. E. Christian (1817-1891), ibid., 183.

12 MNHL MSS 01180 and 01397[A] include more than thirty letters from Moore to G. W. Wood (1889-1907).

13 Joseph Sharples, *Merchant Palaces: Liverpool and Wirral Mansions*, Bluecoat Press, Liverpool, 2007, illustrated with contemporary photographs, gives an idea of the level of luxury enjoyed by wealthy Liverpool businessmen from the 1880s to the First World War, although the Heaps' house, Blackmoor in Eaton Road, is not included. Heap had bought the house in 1881 from the Blessigs, Liverpool cotton merchants of Russian origin, who built it in 1863 in Russian style and called it Peterhof. It was eventually demolished in 1925. www.decisionmodels.com/Blessigs, accessed 19 May 2009.

14 For Mary Louisa Wood (1839-1925), see *New Manx Worthies*, 471-2.

15 Fenella Bazin, *Much Inclin'd to Music: the Manx and Their Music before 1918*, Manx Heritage Foundation, 1997, 108.

16 For Brown's letters to Moore, 1892-7, see MNHL MS 1277/24[A] to 64[A]. The letter quoted is 39[A].

17 *Manx Ballads and Music*, Introduction, xxix.

18 PRO 1/121/6, W. H. Black Memoranda, September 1839, 30, cit. Philippa Levine, op. cit., 110.

19 MNHL 01397[A], Moore to G. W. Wood, 10 August 1891.

20 *Yn Lioar Manninagh*, Vol. II, 1893-4, 78-81.

21 *A History of the Isle of Man*, Vol. II, 685.

22 MNHL MS 1277/43[A], Brown to Moore, 20 February 1895.

Chapter 6 (POLITICIAN, pages 83-98)

1 *Isle of Man Examiner*, 25 July, 1 August 1887.

2 For discussion of this issue, see C. W. Gawne, *The Isle of Man and Britain: Controversy 1651-1895*, Manx Heritage Foundation, 2009.

3 Minute Book of the Manx Museum and Ancient Monuments Trustees, 1886-1918.

4 *Isle of Man Examiner*, 18 April 1891.

5 *Proceedings of Tynwald*, 1891-2; David G. Kermode, *Offshore Island Politics*, Liverpool University Press, 2001, 23-4.

6 Hinton Bird, *An Island That Led: The History of Manx Education, Vol. Two*, Port St Mary, 1995, 60.

7 Derek Winterbottom, *Governors of the Isle of Man Since 1765*, Manx Heritage Foundation, 1999, 106-9.

8 The words in brackets were added later.

9 *Isle of Man Times*, 27 October 1894; *Mona's Herald*, 31 October 1894.

10 *Proceedings of Tynwald*, 1895.

11 There is a contradiction between *Proceedings of Tynwald*, which dates the speech to 30 July, and Moore's diary, which says 15 August, 1896.

12 See the reports on the election in Middle, *Isle of Man Examiner*, 30 January, 6 and 13 February 1897.

13 For John Quine, see autobiographical sketch in MNHL MS 11835; letters from T. E.

Brown to A. W. Moore and John Quine, MNHL MS 1277. For Douglas Grammar School under Quine, see Hinton Bird, op. cit, 81-2.

14 *Proceedings of Tynwald*, House of Keys, 9 December 1898.

Chapter 7 (CELTICIST, pages 99-110)

1 John Belchem, 'The Little Manx Nation: Antiquarianism, Ethnic Identity, and Home Rule Politics in the Isle of Man, 1880-1918', *Journal of British Studies*, 2000, 217-40. The quotation is from page 220.

2 George Broderick, *Language Death in the Isle of Man*, Tübingen, 1999, 46-7.

3 For a sceptical discussion of this subject, see MNHL MS 10382, David Speers, 'Nationalism and Traditional Culture: Celtic Identity and Ideology in the Isle of Man 1890-1940', MA in Manx Studies dissertation, 1999.

4 A. W. Moore, *Surnames and Place-Names of the Isle of Man*, London, 1890, 1-21.

5 Ibid., *The Folk-Lore of the Isle of Man*, Douglas and London, 1891, 1.

6 A. W. Moore and J. Beddoe, 'The Physical Anthropology of the Isle of Man', *Journal of the Anthropological Institute*, August 1897, 104-30.

7 A. W. Moore, *A History of the Isle of Man*, London, 1900, 44-81; quotation from page 44.

8 Sophia Morrison, obituary of A. W. Moore, *Celtic Review*, 16 January 1910, reprinted in *Dictionary of National Biography, 1901-1910*, 1912; ibid., 'The Origin of the Manx Language Society', *Isle of Man Examiner*, 3 January 1914, reprinted in *Manx Quarterly*, September 1914.

9 MNHL MS 11170, Manx Language Society papers, Box 1, William Cubbon, 'The Genesis of the Manx Language Society', typescript of talk, undated but from internal evidence, 1949. Cubbon repeated his claim to have done the initial secretarial work of the MLS in his book, *Island Heritage*, 1952, 322.

10 *Isle of Man Examiner*, 25 March 1899, reprinted as a pamphlet, located in MNHL MS 11170, Box 1.

11 Ibid., 18 November 1899.

12 Ibid., 1 December 1900.

13 *Celtia*, January and June, 1901; 1901 census.

14 This account of the Dublin Congress is based on Quine's notes and on the report in *Celtia*, September 1901.

15 MNHL MS 10847, Manx Language Society papers of J. J. Kneen.

16 Account of the Caernarvon Congress from Quine's notes, and *Celtia*, Summer 1904. See also Marion Löffler, *'A Book of Mad Celts': John Wickens and the Celtic Congress of Caernarfon 1904*, Gomer Press, 2000, in English and Welsh, illustrated with photographs of the Congress.

17 This account is based on Moore's diary and Quine's notes. There may be more to be said about the 1907 Congress, but *Celtic Review* (c.1904-1910), the successor to *Celtia* (1901-5) is not in MNHL and I have not been able to consult it.

18 Compare with John Belchem's interpretation, op.cit.

Chapter 8 (ROYALIST, pages 111-122)

1 See entries in *New Manx Worthies* on Sir James Gell, 183-4, and Deemster Gill's brother W. H. Gill, 201-3.
2 See entry in the *Oxford DNB* for Alice Mary Hughes (1857-1939).
3 Moore's diary for 24-25 August 1909 includes over 2000 words devoted to the royal visit. There is an even longer account, covering much the same ground, in a scrapbook, MNHL MS 09432/1.
4 See George and Weedon Grossmith, *The Diary of a Nobody*, 1892.

Chapter 9 (LAST YEARS, pages 123-146)

1 See MNHL MD 125548, Jeffrey Vaukins, The Manx Struggle for Reform, M.Phil. thesis, Lancaster, 1984.
2 See Samuel Norris, *Manx Memories and Movements*, 1938, reprinted Manx Heritage Foundation, 1994.
3 Lord Raglan (1857-1921), born George Fitzroy Henry Somerset, is not included in the *Oxford DNB*. The nature of his ill-health is unknown. For a useful sketch, see Derek Winterbottom, *Governors of the Isle of Man Since 1765*, Manx Heritage Foundation, 1999, 125-54.
4 For the account of Manx political developments in this chapter, I am largely indebted to David Kermode, *Offshore Island Politics*.
5 See entry for Sir Charles James Symonds (1852-1932) in the *Oxford DNB*.
6 For the sugar tax and reform debates, see *Proceedings of Tynwald*, 29-30 May 1903 and the summary account in Norris, op. cit. 91-5.
7 Full details of the Reform League's 1903 programme are in Norris, op. cit. 371-2.
8 Vaukins, op. cit., 93.
9 *Isle of Man Examiner*, 14 November 1903.
10 *Proceedings of Tynwald*, 6 July 1904.
11 *Isle of Man Examiner*, 12 May 1906.
12 For Armitage Rigby, see *New Manx Worthies*, 411-413.
13 For the text of the 1907 Keys reform petition, see Samuel Norris, op. cit., 373-4.
14 MNHL MS 1180/29[A], A. W. Moore, Queen's Hotel, Birmingham, 12 December 1907, to G. W. Wood.
15 Quine's notes on Arthur Moore's travel diaries become much fuller as they go on. The notes say '31st Camp. See officers of W. Indies Regt. and play polo'. This could be a mistake, but it would be characteristic of Arthur Moore, even at nearly fifty-five, that he would want to join in even if the sport was new to him.
16 National Archives, Home Office papers, H.O. 45/10492/113941/XC 6783, cited in T. W. Cain, 'Constitutional Reform in the Twentieth Century', *Procs. IoMNHAS*, Vol. X, No. 3, 2001-224.
17 T. W. Cain, op. cit., 210.
18 *Isle of Man Examiner*, 14 November 1908.
19 MNHL MS 09495, letters from A.W. Moore to Sophia Morrison, 1885, 1900-1909, with two letters from S. M. to A. W. M., 7 August and 15 October 1909.

Chapter 10 (AFTERWARDS, pages 147-154)

1 The fullest account of the funeral is in the *Isle of Man Examiner*, 20 November 1909, reprinted in *Manx Quarterly*, No. 7, 1909. See also reports in the *Isle of Man Weekly Times*, 20 November 1909, and *Mona's Herald*, 17 November 1909.
2 Will of Arthur William Moore, MNHL J41, 1909/279.
3 *Isle of Man Examiner Annual 1912*, Events of 1911: 11 October and 12 December. See entry on Robert Edward Morrison (1851-1924), in *New Manx Worthies*, 329-30.
4 1891 census; information on Revds John Thomas and Benjamin Clarke from Canon John Gelling, *A History of the Manx Church 1698-1911*, 1998, 225-6.
5 1901 census. Stuart Slack, *Streets of Douglas Old and New*, 1996, 31.
6 Clucas was the returning officer for Middle in the 1903 general election.
7 *Isle of Man Examiner*, 11 November 1908.
8 *Proceedings of Tynwald*, House of Keys, 18 January, 8 November 1910.
9 *King William's College Register*, second edition, 1928, 342.
10 Marriage certificate, Louisa Moore and G. F. Clucas.
11 David Kermode, *Offshore Island Politics*, Liverpool University Press, 2001, 61.
12 Will of Hannah Moore, MNHL J956, 1914/294.
13 MNHL MS 09432/1.
14 *Isle of Man Examiner*, 19 November 1937; *Isle of Man Weekly Times*, 20 November 1937.
15 For Edmund Goodwin, see entry in *New Manx Worthies*, 207-8.
16 Information from Roger Sims.
17 Private information. These books were later returned to the Moore family.
18 MNHL MS 11170, Box 1, William Cubbon, 'The Genesis of the Manx Language Society', 6.
19 MNHL, Minute Book of the Manx Ancient Monuments Trustees, 14 January 1910.
20 John Quine, preface to *Nessy Heywood*, xxvi.

Appendix I (GENEALOGY OF THE MOORES, pages 155-156)

1 During a debate in Tynwald, 16 October 1890, J. T. Cowell said 'With regard to my friend Mr Moore, I have no doubt he is associated with business. I never regarded him as simply a commercial gentleman, but as one who occupied a position by birth'.

Appendix II (MOORE & THE DRINKWATERS, pages 157-159)

1 MNHL MS 09771, including Vanessa Leece Drinkwater, 'The Drinkwaters of the Isle of Man: A Portrait of a Family', undated typescript.
2 See Sir William Leece Drinkwater (1812-1909) in *New Manx Worthies*, 163-4.
3 See letter from George Drinkwater to a doctor about his brother, undated, but from internal evidence written in 1884, included in Vanessa Leece Drinkwater, op. cit.
4 Copy letter in Drinkwater papers, MNHL.

INDEX OF PERSONS

In his diaries, especially when he was young, A. W. Moore often referred to male friends only by their surnames. These surnames have been included in the Index (e.g. BALL, —) even where it has not been possible to identify the person concerned by a first name or initials. Page numbers in *italic* refer to pictures.